GUN-DOG TRAINING
POINTING DOGS

GUN-DOG TRAINING POINTING DOGS

Kenneth C. Roebuck

Photographs and Art Work
David G. Roebuck

Stackpole Books

Published by
STACKPOLE BOOKS
Cameron and Kelker Streets
P.O. Box 1831
Harrisburg, PA 17105

Printed in the U.S.A.

Library of Congress Cataloging in Publication Data

Roebuck, Kenneth C.
   Gun-dog training pointing dogs.

   Includes index.
   1. Hunting dogs.   2. Dogs—Training.   I. Title.
II. Title: Pointing dogs.
SF428.5.R584   1983   636.7'0886   83-4948
ISBN 0-8117-0714-8

*To Joan and David with love
and to Tramp*

Contents

Introduction

THIS BOOK HAS BEEN written to help the hunter train his own pointing dog. So often the owner of a promising puppy has little idea how to go about training it. This book explains how. It covers each stage from choice of breed through buying a puppy, rearing it, starting it right, and teaching it to retrieve, to point staunchly, and to be steady to wing and shot.

The training is conducted in a logical sequence which entails instilling obedience and control first, followed by work on birds later. This way steadiness training becomes a thread weaving its way through the whole process—not something that has to be forced on a dog after it has been encouraged for weeks or months to hunt and chase birds. With the latter, dog *breaking* is being resorted to instead of dog *training*. And therein lies a big difference.

As all dogs are so different in disposition, you will find no daily or weekly training goals in this book. It is simply not possible to train all dogs that way. One's approach to training each individual must be different depending upon its temperament, so it is most important that you study your dog and come to understand his personality before you commence. Learn to "read" him and the chances are good that your efforts to train him will meet with success!

Cardenwood Kennels
Copake, New York
1983

1

Selecting Your Dog

CHOICE OF BREED

Choice of breed, perhaps more than any other factor where pointing dogs are concerned, is a matter you should devote the most careful consideration to if you wish to obtain a gun dog that *you* hunt as opposed to one you tag along somewhere behind while *it* sets the pace. I am referring to the necessity of selecting from stock which possesses the inherent desire to hunt *with* and *for* you, instead of racing away hell-bent for the adjacent county so as to be rarely if ever within sight of you, its handler.

It is an undeniable fact that finding a dog that will hunt close naturally and which, by virtue of this, is not a wide-ranging racing machine, is becoming increasingly difficult in certain breeds. It cannot be denied either that field trialing has, for the most part, caused "big running" to become an inbred trait in many bird dogs, to the extent that, for instance, the desire to retrieve is bred into a labrador.

Field trials for pointing dogs demand that those competing

run hard and range wide. Speed and style and the amount of country covered are the very factors upon which judgment is based, together with, of course, good bird finding and staunch pointing. But it is this desire to range that is the problem today for the man who wishes to hunt slowly through the woods for grouse or the alder thickets for woodcock. Many dogs that will locate and point well (and insofar as these factors are concerned cannot be faulted) will at the same time often hunt at such a distance from the handler as to be completely ineffective under certain hunting conditions. Irritation and frustration thereby result for the owner.

Ranging is fine when hunting quail over great sweeps of flat, open country, sparsely dotted with brush to which a good pointer will make for having recognized it as likely bird-holding cover —provided you are hunting, for instance, in parts of Kansas, Oklahoma, or Nebraska, riding horseback, or driving a jeep to enable you to keep contact with the dog. However, the same dog will be of no use whatever to the grouse or woodcock hunter, as the country over which he is hunting will be such that his dog must keep in close and maintain contact. For this man, a different type of dog altogether is necessary.

I firmly believe that big running in certain breeds—particularly in many lines of pointer and setter and, fast catching up with them, some German shorthaired pointers—is so inbred now as to be virtually impossible to reliably and permanently correct, no matter what methods (many of which I consider questionable) are employed. In the end the bottom line is quite simply this: The manner in which a dog hunts is influenced by the way it is bred. At one end of the scale there are those bred just for the show ring that will not hunt at all, and at the other, those bred to be field trialed that invariably turn out big runners. And they run big because that is what they are bred to do, and field trialing demands it of them.

This ranging can sometimes be controlled, at least to a certain extent, by experienced handling and the manner in which a dog is taught to quarter. The term quarter means to hunt ahead of and to each side of the handler in such a manner that the ground is hunted to best possible effect. This ensures that as little game as possible is missed. But in general, converting such a dog to be a permanently reliable close worker is virtually impossible.

It is essential therefore that, where choice of breed is being considered, the problem of big running be one that all potential gun-dog owners are aware of, in order that they can make every effort to avoid buying from lines in which this trait is so strongly ingrained.

Being specific about what steps to take to ensure that one obtains the right type of dog is difficult at best. All I can recommend is that thorough inquiries be made of as many professional trainers as possible and that one make it abundantly clear that it is a *gun dog* and not a *field trial dog* that one is seeking. Explain that you are looking for a dog that will have the natural tendency to stay within an acceptable distance while hunting.

German shorthaired pointer.

Hungarian vizsla.

English setter.

Wirehaired pointing griffon.

Breeders do exist who have made every effort over the years to retain close working tendencies in their dogs. These breeders are usually keen hunters, particularly of grouse and woodcock, who have never been actively involved in trialing but who nevertheless produce good cover-bashing, bird-finding dogs— setters, for instance.

Brittanies, Hungarian vizslas, and wirehaired pointing griffons, for instance, usually exhibit the desire to hunt *for* you and to do so within reasonable range, thereby eliminating undue strain on your blood pressure! The same applies to German wirehaired pointers. Yet I hate generalizing where dogs are concerned, especially when discussing different breeds.

Pointer.

Making thorough inquiries from those who train is therefore going to be your best approach, while taking into consideration what type of hunting you do and where you do it. Sound advice is usually forthcoming from professional trainers, if approached properly; provided they train the breeds you are interested in, they are best suited to understand your needs.

In my previous book (*Gun-Dog Training: Spaniels and Retrievers*) I stated that I think it advisable to choose the type of dog that "most pleases your eye," as he's going to be a part of the family for some time to come. I stress this again, as it is better to do this than to get one whose appearance you may never be entirely happy about. But make no mistake—it is most essential that you take working ability into consideration first and foremost.

And bear in mind this, too: Don't think that, because you

Brittany spaniel.

Brittany spaniel (tri-color; French-bred)

hunted with Old Joe's German shorthair or setter or brittany, as good a dog as it may have been, if you go out and obtain one of the same breed you will be assured of getting a dog possessing the same working characteristics. The chances of this are extremely remote. There are no two dogs alike, either in appearance or temperament, not even those from the same litter. All dogs, like us, are individuals.

So inquire from people who know and, having got sound advice, act upon it.

PICKING A PUPPY

We will presume that choice of breed has been decided upon and that you have located a breeder who produces the type of dog you require. The best age to take home a puppy is around seven to eight weeks. By then it will have been weaned for the last two weeks or so and have been eating puppy food from a dish. By this age individual personalities have begun to form and it is possible to get a fairly good idea of disposition and general appearance. In this respect, I place the desirability of a good, sound disposition at the top of my list every time.

Feeding time. Belle, an English setter.

Future gun dogs. Seven-week-old brittany spaniels bred from French blood-lines. Note the black-and-white puppy.

Start by taking a look at the dam, and the sire too if he is around. He's not always there, of course, as someone else may own him. Check overall appearance as well as disposition. In addition, satisfy yourself that the circumstances in which the pups have been reared are like those in which you would want to rear a litter of your own.

Next, take a look at the pups and remove from the whelping box or run only those you are interested in; that is, males or

Take out of the dog run only those you are interested in selecting from.

females. And a few words about this aspect while we are on the subject. Choice of male or female is entirely personal and is a matter about which little advice can be given by anyone. Your home circumstances may dictate which you must choose. However, bear this in mind: Insofar as working ability is concerned, provided disposition and breeding are both sound, one sex should be no better a hunter than the other as both are capable of making equally good gun dogs. I tend to find that females are inclined to be "with you" mentally more than males. They usually want to please more, whereas many males are inclined to be independent and (yes, it's true!) hardheaded at times. But this is only a personal view.

Most people's thoughts in coming to this decision revolve around one of the following notions: (1) I'll get a female because I'd like to have just one litter of pups, then I'll get her spayed, or (2) if I get a female, I'll have the problem of her coming into season twice a year and I don't want her to have pups, as this could be a nuisance; also spayed females get fat and don't hunt as well.

My answers to these two points of view are as follows: (1) Never have a litter of pups from a bitch simply because you think it might be fun. It isn't always so. It can in fact result in a lot of hard work, particularly when they start feeding independently. In addition, you may not be able to sell them easily when they get to the appropriate age. Pups given away are never appreciated as much as pups purchased, simply because the recipient may never have really intended having one. The least any dog deserves is a good home. And lastly, the chances are you will make little or nothing financially for your trouble. (2) If you do prefer a female, then go ahead and get one despite your worries about her coming into season. If this would affect your hunting or if you fear she may get bred accidentally, the solution is simple. Wait until she has been in season for the first time, at around nine months of age, then have her spayed. By doing this you are eliminating both possibilities—permanently.

Having your dog spayed will not adversely affect her desire to hunt nor will she become fat as a result of the operation. She will become fat only from overeating; a sensible diet will ensure that she keeps her figure.

Now let's get back to actually choosing the pup. As I suggested earlier, separate those pups in which you are interested, then weed out all but two or three from which to make your final choice. First, look for signs of a good, sound disposition. In other words, try to find a puppy which approaches you boldly and with confidence, showing no fear. Disregard any which cower or run away and hide and which are afraid to come up to you. This indicates nervousness which is unlikely to disappear and may even get worse during its adult life.

With spaniels and retrievers, I advocate a little retrieving test using a rolled-up handkerchief or similar object; it can also be useful to try this with pointing breeds. Some will have little interest in trying to retrieve. To be sure, the best future retriever of the lot may be the pup showing the least interest at that particular time because of a recent feed and a full stomach. Nevertheless the test is interesting to try as it may reveal a desire to pick up and carry and also show confidence and inquisitiveness in approaching and investigating something strange and new.

Don't automatically ignore the smallest pup either, just because it *is* the smallest. Size is of little consequence where desire to hunt is concerned. If the pup exhibits the same boldness as the others and appears to be just as healthy, take it into account also. I've known many smallest pups to develop into fine gun dogs.

Carefully look over each pup you are considering and make sure the eyes are clear and bright. The coat should not be dull but sleek and healthy in appearance. Ensure too that the dew claws have been removed. These are located on the inside of the legs, sometimes on all four, sometimes on just two. They tend to grow in a complete circle if not removed and later are inclined to tear on cover while the dog is hunting. Evolution has meant that they are now no longer of any practical use to a dog. This excision, together with tail-docking for those breeds to which the latter applies, should have been dealt with by a veterinarian or the breeder when the pups were no more than three or four days old.

When choosing a puppy of any recognized breed of hunting dog, it is very important if that puppy is to be a future gun dog that it be bred from good, sound hunting bloodlines. To establish

Check that the eyes are clear and that the coat is sleek and in healthy condition.

this, take a look at a four- or five-generation pedigree of the sire and dam. If you don't know enough about pedigrees, take someone with you who can decipher them for you.

No pup should be considered a potential gun dog if bred entirely from "show-bench" lines. Dogs of 100-percent show breeding are invariably used only to exhibit in the show ring, so the chances of getting a good gun dog from such a source are extremely remote.

There is in fact a balance to be found in breeding between the 100-percent show dog and the 100-percent field trialer from which the gun-dog man should try to make his selection. It is important that this be made clear as we are concerned in this book with dogs for the man who hunts and who wants a reliable and easy-to-handle dog in the field. It is his interest that must be served and for me to ignore these very valid points would do him an injustice.

On making your final selection, be sure to ask when the pup was last wormed and what for. It is quite likely that worming will have to be carried out again, probably at least twice more, as worms, no matter of what type, can be extremely difficult to clear.

Ask also what shots, if any, they have had and make a note

of precisely what type was used and whether or not this included inoculation for parvovirus. The latter has been essential since this new canine problem appeared a few years ago. On getting home follow up by having a local vet give whatever additional shots are necessary and take with you the information on what the pup has already been given. In the meantime, until he is fully protected keep him away from other dogs in the neighborhood.

Finally, make sure that when you get your puppy you also get from the breeder the registration papers. These will be evidence for registration either in *The Field Dog Stud Book* in Chicago or at the American Kennel Club in New York, depending upon what breed you have bought. The main point is that the papers should have been applied for and issued by the registering authority to the breeder in time to be handed over with the puppy. Sometimes this is not possible and there is a genuine reason for the delay. If the breeder hasn't yet received them, it is advisable to get a note with your receipt guaranteeing that the papers will be forwarded to you as soon as they are received by him.

So you now have a prospective gun dog and you are on your way home with your prized possession and thoughts of days afield, points, retrieves, and lots of birds to come.

However, a word of advice in this respect: What *you* do from this day on with your puppy will influence him for better or worse for the rest of his life.

CONSIDERING A TRAINED DOG

Although this book is about how to train a gun dog yourself, it will also be useful to the person who has chosen to buy a started or fully trained dog instead. The very same principles of training apply and can be followed either to complete the dog's training or, in the case of one already fully trained, to keep it up to standard.

Some people prefer to take this course rather than to buy a puppy and take the risk—which certainly does exist—of rearing it for eight to ten months only to find that it isn't going to make the grade. No matter how good the breeding, there can be no guarantee how any individual pup may turn out. Let's face it—you, the owner, may ruin it!

Those who prefer to buy a trained or started dog look at things from the point of view that (a) they can see what its appearance is like now that it's fully grown, and (b) more important, they can see how well it works. This way most of the risk is eliminated. Adopting this approach can therefore be a perfectly sound way of obtaining a good gun dog, but there are pitfalls, so allow me to give you a few words of advice should this be contemplated.

Never, under any circumstances, should you consider buying a trained or started dog without first watching it being worked by the person selling it. If asked, the trainer or owner should willingly demonstrate to you all that it is claimed the dog will do. If the owner hedges or makes excuses, don't touch the dog with a ten-foot pole. If it is too far to go to see a dog, then shop elsewhere, but be reasonably prepared to travel; good gun dogs don't grow on trees! You are buying a future hunting companion that will be a part of your days afield for years to come—not some inanimate object like a shirt or a pair of boots that you can safely get by mail order.

Do not be talked into having a dog shipped to you on approval unless you know very well the person selling it and have had satisfactory dealings with him before. This expedient can result in problems, financial and otherwise, that you wouldn't have thought possible.

Be prepared also to pay a fair price for a good dog. Do not expect that the price today will resemble what you paid for "Old Blue" fourteen years ago. Times have changed and so has the cost of living; trainers, like everyone else, have to try to cope with it. Months or maybe even a year or two will have been spent achieving what you see in a dog, so be prepared to pay what it's worth.

Having bought your dog and got him home, don't be tempted to take him out in the field the very next day. You must allow him time to settle down and get accustomed to you and his new home. Remember, he doesn't know you, the house is strange, his surroundings are unfamiliar, and he is going to be puzzled for a while as to what is going on. You will have to spend a few days at first walking and talking to him and getting to know him, and he you. Feeding him yourself will help a great deal, as will lots of kind words and having him in your company as much as possible. Most dogs with good sound temperaments settle easily after two or three days. You will sense when this has come about. Prior to this, it is advisable to keep him leashed while you walk him. It would be a disaster if he got lost.

If a whistle has been used in your dog's training, be sure to get from the trainer the same type he used. This will help enormously when working him as it will in any event take time for him to get accustomed to your tone of voice and the manner in which you give commands. No two people handle a dog in exactly the same way.

Lastly, another aspect of buying a trained dog that you should be fully aware of: No matter how well-trained the dog is you must realize that you may never be able to gain the same sharp, attentive, obedient response from it that the trainer himself did. You may assume that this is because (a) he trained it, (b) it knows him well, and (c) he's had the dog longer. Right to a certain extent, but not entirely! There are other factors. More likely than not the reasons will be that (a) you are inexperienced, and (b) you lack the natural ability to be at all times "at one" with a dog. Not everyone possesses the ability to handle a dog well and hold its attention and respect; for those who do not, no amount of advice or instruction will ever improve matters.

When showing a dog working, a trainer is demonstrating what he has trained the dog to do and how it works for *him*. He cannot be responsible for how it works for its new owner because all his help and advice at the time of the sale may in fact be

The author's training kennel.

largely ignored. A dog is an animal capable of showing either affection or distrust, of being obedient or disobedient, and of hunting under control or running riot if its handler does not give and enforce commands in a firm and timely manner. Your own ability and determination to keep your dog the way it was when you bought it is what counts in the end.

So it's up to you! If things don't work out as they should have, then it is almost certainly your fault, not the dog's.

The choice, therefore, as to whether you buy a puppy or a fully trained or started dog is yours alone. But whatever your decision I trust this book will help you either to train it to a standard you have admired in other people's dogs or to maintain your trained dog at the level it had reached when you bought it.

FEEDING

Selection of the proper food is perhaps the easiest aspect of keeping a dog and a far cry from the choices available thirty years ago. Many brands of good dog meal can be bought from pet stores and supermarkets everywhere. Today any manufacturer has to be good if he wishes to survive the competition.

I prefer the all-in-one type of meal which contains all the vitamins and minerals a dog needs. However, there is no reason why leftovers from meals should not be added, such as meat, gravy, and vegetables. Such foods relieve the monotony of the exact same thing each feed.

For the first two or three months (from the time the puppy is weaned at five weeks of age) I suggest a well-proven puppy meal. This should be soaked in hot water, then left to stand for fifteen minutes or so before being fed. A broth can be used instead of water if preferred. Later, when the pup is feeding well —say, from eight to ten weeks of age—this type of food can also be provided dry on a self-feed basis, i.e., by leaving a bowl of feed there all the time so that it can help itself as it wishes. But if this method is used you should be sure that there is always a bowl of water alongside the feed, as most dogs on the dry, self-feed method tend to drink more. There can be a drawback though: Some dogs will gorge themselves. In this case the practice is best discontinued and the soaked-feed method substituted.

A puppy on a soaked-feed diet should be fed three times daily until it is around five months old, twice daily until seven months old, then once daily from that time on. Careful observation for the first week or so will soon give you an idea how much feed he needs. Remember your puppy is growing all the time, so be sure he gets enough to encourage good growth.

I strongly advise against giving bones to dogs, at least most types of bones. They may taste good and the dog may enjoy them, but they can be dangerous. Any bone that will crack and split open is a potential hazard; splinters may get stuck in the throat or the intestines and you can very quickly have a dead dog. Under no circumstances should fish or poultry bones be given as they are perhaps the most dangerous of all. Some people will give soft bones in the belief that they can't possibly do any harm. Wrong! They can indeed. Enough of these can result in blocked intestines, from which death can quickly result.

About the only safe bones are the large knuckle bones. This type can be chewed and gnawed on but rarely split open other than by a large, powerfully built dog. Puppies will spend hours blissfully grinding away at one, which not only tends to preserve the woodwork in the kennel or the furniture in the home, but also cleans teeth and strengthens jaws. Do not be tempted to give any other type and never give one bone to two dogs, for obvious reasons.

HUMANIZING

All puppies benefit by going to their new home at around seven or eight weeks of age, as they can at this very early age become more easily accustomed to the sights and sounds of everyday life. Since three to four weeks of age a puppy's brain has been developing rapidly. Intelligence and emotions have started to form and the animal has become gradually more aware of its surroundings. Lack of human contact now can create a lack of confidence in humans later. As every dog inherits the pack instinct, it is, at this age, prepared to accept dominance from its master. Therefore, with proper handling it will develop a strong sense of security.

Any puppy that is treated as part of the family is automatically exposed to the everyday comings and goings in the home. Not only is he getting to know the different members of the family but he is also meeting and being handled by friends and neighbors, adults and children. And he is soon introduced to the outside world by being taken for walks in the area.

All the things which we regard as normal and everyday are at first somewhat daunting to any young dog. It is in this period of his very early life that this process is most effective and will have a lasting influence on adult behavior. You can be sure that he will accept all the sudden changes in his life far more easily now than would an older dog which had been isolated in a kennel with little or no human contact, other than being fed, for the first few months of life.

I have one strong reservation relating to the *sounds* aspect. I refer to the overanxious owner's wanting to find out whether his pup is gun-shy. Do not be tempted, as many people unfortunately are, to take your puppy to the local trap-and-skeet club and walk him on the leash along the back of a line of twelve-gauge shotguns being discharged. This could prove disastrous. My answer to people who claim that they did this without adverse effects is that they were very fortunate indeed, and they almost certainly will not be so lucky with the next one. Rest assured, any puppy that is not gun-nervous when you get there probably will be by the time you leave, though you may not realize it. It is simply not worth the risk. Introduction to gunfire is a separate exercise which should be conducted carefully and sensibly under the right circumstances. If it is carried out properly, you eliminate the risks. More on this later.

Your puppy should have plenty of free-running exercise but by this I do not mean that he should be allowed to take off into the fields and woods on his own. I mean free-running exercise in your company. Dogs turned loose to "self-hunt" will later hunt only for themselves and not for their handler, and serious control problems will result.

Allow your puppy off the leash while walking in the fields and woods and, as he gets a little older and bolder, walk him through the deeper and thicker places to accustom him to getting into bird-holding cover. Right now is the very best time to teach him to keep in good and close. It is of no use whatever to expect any hunting dog to stay close while hunting if, when exercising him, you allow him to range far and wide as he pleases. Establishing control means being consistent. So take along the whistle and start getting him used to it in the way I advise in chapter 4 in the section on "Quartering."

Playtime with pups is important, too, and can be made much more interesting by allowing the puppy to chase and pick up and carry something. At this stage the object used need not be a retrieving dummy, nor is it necessary to exercise any control either. You are merely allowing him to enjoy fetching and carrying.

This can be done in the yard, in your basement, or even in the house if you want. A glove, slipper, or old hat will do just fine as long as he will pick it up and carry it around. By all means get him into the habit of bringing it back to you, but don't overdo it. Three or four throws are quite enough for one session. And when he does get to you with it, don't snatch it away. Take hold of it, stroke his head and praise him, and gently remove it from his mouth while saying "Leave."

What you are actually doing, without his realizing it, is starting to teach the retrieve exercise. This will help considerably when you get around to doing this more seriously and under more control later.

2

Choice of Housing

YOUR HOME OR A KENNEL

Opinions vary in relation to whether a potential gun dog should live in a kennel or in the home. My recommendation is always to compromise. Have a doghouse and dog run for him out in the yard, but also allow him into the home when you are around, as often as you are able. As I have said earlier, I believe it to be very important that a puppy get the kind of attention in the home which it would seriously miss if it were isolated in a kennel all the time. The more a puppy is in your company the more it will relate to you; in turn, as time goes on you will have a more attentive dog, one that will want to please you more. Moreover, being allowed to play with children instills a lot of confidence in any puppy and, provided common sense is exercised, nothing but good will result.

On the other hand, if it simply isn't possible to bring the pup into the home you can, alternatively, make every effort to take it out for runs as often as you can and spend time with it in and

30

Natasha, a Hungarian vizsla. Keeping a gun dog in the home will not adversely affect its working ability.

around your yard. It is essential to ensure that the pup isn't ignored and left alone to brood for days on end. As long as it comes into contact with you each day and is taken out of the kennel for free exercise, it will do well.

I certainly prefer that any dog be in a doghouse with a run rather than simply in a doghouse on a chain. I detest the latter arrangement and would never recommend it to anyone.

Try, therefore, to have your pup in the home part of the time and in the kennel the other part. If you do not have the room to erect a kennel and run, just keep him in the house with you. If you are sensible it will work out fine.

HOUSE TRAINING

For people who have to keep their puppy in the home or who regularly bring it into the home from the kennel during the day or evening, house training is essential, and the amount of effort that you, the owner, put into teaching it will be the measure of its success or failure.

House training is best started the very day you take your puppy home. In general, pups are inclined to be quite clean in their habits and, when still in the whelping box at four to five weeks old, will walk to the opposite end of the box from their customary sleeping area to relieve themselves.

It helps, at least until house training has been completed, to restrict the puppy to a specific area in your home; for instance, the kitchen or porch. If it is allowed to wander at will, puddles will begin to appear on your best carpets and rugs, and it will be difficult for the puppy to learn better manners.

The kitchen is often most suitable because of the usual type of floor covering, which enables cleaning to be carried out more easily when accidents occur. A small pen can be used; for example, a child's playpen or a commercially made, collapsible type constructed of welded wire mesh. You should ensure that its size is adequate in relation to the size and age of the pup, allowing it sufficient room to walk around freely. It is desirable not to resort to the use of newspapers; a positive effort right from the start to take him out regularly to relieve himself in the garden is the best technique. The presence of papers in the pen tends to confuse the issue and prolong the process, as the puppy will associate them with those which used to be in his whelping box to relieve himself on. This will tend to negate the effort he would otherwise make to indicate to you that he wants to go out. If trained correctly, most pups very quickly start to do this.

From this time on everything depends on your willingness to act quickly and take him out to the same area of the yard each time he shows signs of wanting to relieve himself; that is, when he starts to turn in circles and sniff around urgently. You can be sure he will want to go after a feed, on waking up at any time, and before being left alone for the night. You should also take him out to the same area frequently even when he doesn't show signs of wanting to go.

It is also a good idea to get the puppy used to a command which he will associate with this function. I usually say "Be quick" and have found that, if it is said each time he goes, he soon comes to understand what is meant and reacts accordingly. He will literally, in time, go to the bathroom on request.

Do not be tempted to let a puppy wander off on his own outside just because of your reluctance to brave inclement weather conditions. He may soil the doorstep, or you may allow him back into the house not knowing whether the object of his excursion has been achieved or he simply had a wonderful time exercising the neighbor's cat. Going out with him for those first two or three weeks is the only way.

Time of feeding, too, will almost certainly affect his ability to last through the night. This can only be solved by trial and error but, as a general rule, if he is taken out conscientiously the very last thing at night, the chances are good that all will be well until morning.

Once things appear to be working, you can remove the pen and permit him to roam around a little more. By now you may find that he will naturally restrict himself to the kitchen area, which probably will suit you fine. Watch carefully though for some time to prevent accidents from happening. It is quite likely that by now he will be making his own way towards the door, thereby indicating his desire to go out.

If an accident does happen, do not be tempted, no matter what the circumstances, to punish the puppy after some time has elapsed, as it is extremely unlikely that he will be able to associate a scolding with what he has done wrong. Corrective measures are only effective when a dog is caught in the act, at which time he should be picked up, scolded, and taken right out to the usual area of the yard. And however tempted due to your anger, do not resort to rubbing the pup's nose in his feces. This is a very bad practice and may result in his starting to eat his own stools, since he must of course lick his nose to clean himself.

Puppies have very short memories and corrective action should only be administered at the time an offense is committed. If it is too late, there is nothing you can do but try to be more prepared next time.

House training often is a rather tedious and frustrating process but, if carried out correctly for a couple of weeks or so, it will work.

MAKING OR BUYING A DOG RUN

To house one dog, a run should be of a minimum size of, say, six feet wide by six feet high by twelve feet long. If you wish to make it yourself, it can be constructed by using treated four-by-fours. These should be made into frames, each six feet square, on which a good-quality, two-inch welded mesh wire can be stretched and stapled into position. The wire comes in rolls six feet high. Each section should be strengthened by securing a cross section made from the same diameter wood at the three-foot level, and metal supports should be screwed across each corner as well as at top and bottom to hold the frame rigid. Each section including the gate, which should be made in the same manner, can then be fastened with carriage bolts. This way you have a good, strong, portable dog run that can easily be taken apart and relocated should you later decide to move your home.

The alternative is to buy a dog run from one of the many companies which manufacture and ship them. Complete panel sections and gates can be obtained which are made from steel piping with wire already stretched and secured to the frames, after which most are galvanized. Each section of the run is then fastened very easily with clamps and bolts, and the assembly can be erected in thirty minutes or so.

I recommend this type of dog run because it is not chewable like wood. It looks good and, if taken care of, will last a lifetime. Where woodwork is concerned I have found that some dogs can do more damage than a family of beavers! If a second run of the same type is ever required, it can be bolted right onto the side of the first as everything is made to standard size.

Insofar as run surfaces are concerned I usually suggest concrete, although it can be difficult to keep clean under cold and icy conditions. If this material is used, the base should be made to extend about two feet wider than the dog run itself all the way around, and the run should not be cemented in. Custom-made sections come with a number of two-inch-high feet which clamp to the bottom pipe. This keeps the metal run off the concrete and thus helps preserve it from the corrosive effects of urine and water.

A concrete slab should be thick enough to withstand hard frosts and should be reinforced with a steel-mesh insert. This

An efficient two-run dog kennel.

These are custom-made runs which clamp together, providing plenty of room for one dog in each.

will help reduce the chances of cracking.

A good alternative to cement is pea gravel. It washes well and looks clean provided you keep the gravel replenished. This means always having a supply on hand because it is inevitable that, each time you clean out droppings, which should be done at least twice daily, you will throw out some gravel, too. Earth runs should never be used as they become muddy and get in a terrible state in wet weather; they also tend to harbor worm eggs and other parasites far more than does concrete or gravel. Thorough cleaning simply isn't possible with an earth run.

Concrete runs should be hosed down and disinfected regularly, although this can pose a big problem in the northern states in extremely cold weather. Gravel runs cannot be hosed down in the same way, of course, so it is necessary at least once a week to disinfect such runs with a good kennel disinfectant or with diluted Clorox, which will kill just about any germ or worm eggs that happen to be there. The disinfectant should be sprinkled liberally over the gravel with a watering can. But be sure to check that the solution you intend to use is suitable for kennels and will not cause sickness in the animals.

A bucket of fresh drinking water should always be hanging by a snap catch inside the run. The water should be changed daily. In summer galvanized buckets can be used but in winter the thick rubber, agricultural type is preferable. When water freezes solid overnight in metal buckets it can burst them wide open at the seams; this will not happen with rubber ones.

One essential thing to bear in mind prior to setting up the doghouse and run is to choose a nice shady spot if you possibly can. Avoid locating the doghouse in such a position that in summer the sun is beating down on it during the hottest time of day. Also try to position it so that the entrance faces away from the prevailing winter winds.

In this connection, people tend to worry about dogs in cold weather. They need not, provided the dog has a good, dry, draft-proof house with suitable bedding, such as cedar shavings or oat straw. The time to be really concerned is the hottest part of summer when the temperature may reach the nineties. Heat prostration can kill a dog far more quickly than you would think possible. But how many dogs do you know that hate snow?

BUILDING A DOGHOUSE

Using the type of dog run I have suggested, you can arrange things in one of two ways.

(1) The run can be secured to the side of an existing building, such as a barn, a shed, or your garage, in which the doghouse will be located. If this is done the back section of the run will not be required. It will be necessary to cut into the side of the building, a few inches above ground level, an entrance about twelve inches by sixteen inches to allow the dog access from the run. You can then install, if you wish, a two-way swinging door to help eliminate drafts. Inside the building a run similar to but smaller than that outside can be installed; in it should be placed a wooden bed three feet square. It should also have six-inch sides all around, and wooden blocks should be secured to the underside in order to raise it two or three inches off the floor.

Next, another box two feet, six inches high should be made— this time with no base but only a top. This should be large enough to fit snugly over the bed. Cut into it at the end farthest from the entrance into the building should be a hole to give the dog access. This box is where the dog will sleep and the idea of the separate top is to permit its removal for periodic washing and disinfecting. This would be impossible if it were permanently secure.

You now have a good, draft-proof house inside the building which, with bedding put in for winter, will be warm and snug for any dog even in the severest weather. In spring and summer no bedding is necessary as more likely than not he'll sleep on top of the box or even out in the run. The bed itself and the box cover can be made from five-eighths plywood. Exterior ply will not be necessary as the setup will be inside the building permanently.

(2) If, on the other hand, you prefer to have a separate doghouse, one can be made fairly easily. It can either stand inside the run or be positioned on the outside tight up against the side of the run, with a hole cut in the wire so the dog can enter the house. This time, though, use exterior-grade plywood. The doghouse need be no more than, say, four feet wide by three feet

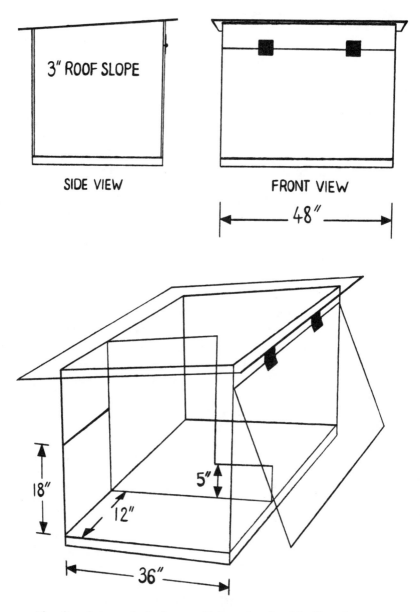

3" ROOF SLOPE

SIDE VIEW

FRONT VIEW

48"

18"

12"

5"

36"

Plan for a homemade doghouse which can be placed inside a dog run.

deep with a slight slope of the roof from front to back to allow water to run off. If the doghouse is going to stand inside the run, the entrance should be located at the back, about twelve by sixteen inches in size, and should be close to one side.

A draft board should be fitted to the full height of the house and three quarters of its depth. This will then have formed a corridor one foot wide along which the dog will walk before going around the end into the sleeping section. The entire front panel of the house (opposite the entrance) can be made in the form of a door hinged either at the top or at one side, so that it can be opened to permit cleaning. It can also be left open in hot weather. One should secure to the bottom of the house four-by-fours all around to raise it off the ground. Be sure to shingle the roof or cover it with good-quality tar paper. In northern states, serious consideration should be given to double walls, roof, and floor with insulation between.

If you locate the doghouse inside the run, remember that a dog can easily jump onto the roof, which in turn places him in an ideal position to leap over the side and out of the run. It is therefore advisable to cover the top of the run with a roll of chicken wire. Better safe than sorry!

I think it a good idea too, especially in the northern states, to have a snow panel the full width of the gate. For instance, in a six-foot-high run this means having a permanently fixed, one-foot panel above which will be a five-foot-high gate. This is so that in heavy snow the bottom of the gate will not get buried, causing a nuisance if freezing occurs. It will eliminate a lot of unnecessary digging, too.

Equipment

TRAINING-KIT LIST

Following is a list of equipment it is advisable to have:

(1) One four-foot leather or nylon leash with choke chain
(2) A nylon slip-leash for the pocket
(3) A thirty-foot check line with a leash snap on the end
(4) A whistle, preferably plastic, with a lanyard for carrying it round the neck
(5) A waterproof canvas dummy
(6) A .22-caliber blank training pistol
(7) A pigeon-sized bird-release cage

I shall discuss the check line first and then take up the quail call-back pen, which, although not listed as a necessity, is nevertheless most useful if quail are going to be employed at all. I shall also express my personal views on electronic training devices, which, you will notice, do *not* appear on my equipment list.

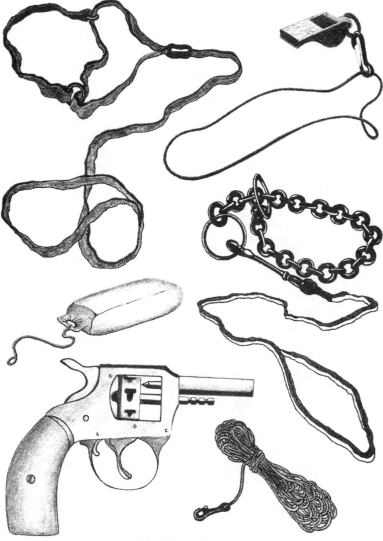

Training equipment.

THE CHECK LINE

This item of equipment is simply a strong, light rope which can be of any length, but I suggest that thirty feet or so is long

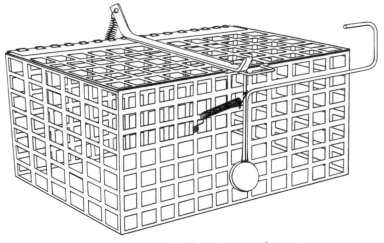

Release cage suitable for pigeon or pheasant.

enough. It can prove most useful when problems are encountered in teaching a dog to "whoa" or in the recall, staunchness on point, or steadiness to wing and shot. It can be a help, too, when teaching a dog to hunt closer and to develop a good quartering pattern. No useful purpose is served by going into more detail now regarding how the check line should be used when particular problems are encountered since, throughout the book, as each stage is reached, I refer to the check line and its relative usefulness to that particular exercise.

I firmly maintain though that a dog which has been guided correctly through the training procedure at its own pace from the time it is young should rarely if ever need the check line. Your control over the dog should by that time be up to such a standard that he respects you and thereby reacts to your commands willingly.

If the use of the check line is resorted to excessively its value decreases, as dogs quickly come to realize when the check line is on and when it is not, and therefore when they can get away with things and when they cannot. If it is used too often and suddenly left off, the dog will almost certainly take advantage of the situation, knowing you no longer have that same magical control over him. Used as little as possible, therefore, with corrective measures applied in a timely and forceful manner, the check line will be far more effective than when used on a long-term, routine basis.

With older dogs—those perhaps twelve months old or more, especially those that have experienced little or no yard-work training—it is a different story. Such dogs can be a problem as they have been subjected to no discipline and have pretty well been able to please themselves throughout a very impressionable period of their life. Starting to enforce discipline at this age therefore presents a trainer with a different set of circumstances altogether, and resort to the use of the check line becomes a virtual necessity; a certain independence has been formed which necessitates a much firmer approach.

Lastly, another very good reason why use of the check line should be avoided if possible is that, when being dragged by the dog, the line seems to become tangled around every bush and tree you come across, not to mention your own and the dog's legs. Thus it can be more of a nuisance than it is worth and, I repeat, should not be necessary for a young dog correctly started.

THE QUAIL CALL-BACK PEN

Bobwhite quail are an ideal bird on which to train pointing dogs provided they are released regularly from a call-back pen so that they retain their ability to fly strongly. On the other hand, quail reared under conditions which do not allow them to fly and thereby exercise and strengthen their wings, as by being housed in a good, long flight pen, make poor training aids as they quickly weaken when released. After a couple of flights they are easily caught by a dog. The use of quail for training is further discussed in chapter 7.

Quail call-back pens vary considerably in size and style. There are those, for instance, which are so large as to require two people to move them. This type is usually made with a wood frame and constructed on two levels, one section above the other, each with an enclosed house at the end which is usually made of plywood. Handles at the ends enable the pen to be lifted and moved. Half-inch wire mesh on two-by-two wooden framing is

The check line is often a useful item of equipment when training young dogs.

A portable two-tier quail call-back pen.

Close-up of reentry tunnel to lower tier.

usually employed. A pen this size can comfortably house twelve to fifteen birds. In the lower section, on one side only, is a wire entrance tunnel generally made from hardware cloth. This reentry tunnel should be about four-and-a-half inches in diameter at the entrance, tapering to about three-and-a-half inches (not less) inside, at which point it is secured by a length of wire to the wire floor of the section above so that it slopes up slightly. This means that when quail enter along the tunnel, they drop down inside the pen. This ensures that they cannot exit the same way as the end is above the height at which they walk around inside the pen. In the top section of the pen, one or two cock birds are always left as call-back birds so that their calling in late afternoon or evening will entice those released earlier in the day to return.

Food and water should be available at all times on both levels. This is put in through doors the full width of the pen, one for each level, each usually hinged at the bottom. Quail like greens with normal quail feed; chick grit should also be placed in the pen in a separate bowl. The overall size of a pen of this type should be approximately seven-and-a-half feet long by three feet wide by three feet deep.

Much smaller portable call-back pens can be constructed to hold about six to eight birds so that they can be carried easily by one person from place to place. These have only one level and can be made with a light wooden frame and the same wire mesh and entrance tunnel. If preferred, the small house at the end which merely provides protection in bad weather can be made so that it and the pen are two separate units, which can be bolted or hooked together when set in place. This can be advantageous when they are moved fairly regularly. There are also even lighter-weight, all-wire models which can easily be purchased from sporting goods suppliers.

For the one- or two-dog owner, the smaller, lightweight type is adequate as six to eight quail if looked after can last a whole training season or longer.

Also in chapter 7 I'll talk about chukar partridge (which can be used from the same pen) and pigeons, the latter being in certain respects the best bird to use for much of the basic training anyway.

ELECTRONIC TRAINING DEVICES

My personal views relating to the use of electronic devices for the training of dogs are very uncomplicated. Quite frankly I deplore their use for routine training although I do acknowledge that the electronic collar, if used by a trainer who thoroughly understands the principles of its application, can be a useful aid in correcting one or two particularly serious faults, such as bolting (running off unpredictably for great distances) and deer chasing.

It would appear to me, I regret to say, that we have now entered an era in which many trainers, professional as well as amateur, appear to think that these devices are essential. And I for one think it is a pretty sad state of affairs.

If the use of an electronic collar has to be resorted to at all, I think it should be used only to help correct serious faults of the type I have already mentioned, for which no other solution has been effective. I don't believe an electronic device of any kind should ever be necessary to train a dog which has been brought up correctly and has the desire to hunt, point, and (hopefully) retrieve. Why on earth anyone should use electric cattle prods on dogs is beyond me. A cattle prod is a hand-held instrument which is applied directly to an animal. If the dog is so close to the handler that it can be given a shock, then why use it at all? Surely, under such circumstances, other corrective measures can be employed.

There are no shortcuts to training a dog well and certainly the use of electronic devices by an inexperienced trainer, who is, after all, learning himself, should not be considered. There is no doubt that many potentially good gun dogs are ruined by the owner's loss of temper and the resulting improper use of such devices.

Starting Right

THE PSYCHOLOGICAL APPROACH

Understanding the basic principles of the psychological approach to dog training is so important that it deserves detailed explanation, as most difficulties encountered while training probably arise from the inability of the owner to "read" the canine mind.

Put simply, when training any dog there are times when corrective action should be taken for doing wrong, and there are times when praise must be given for doing right. This is a basic rule of training and one that most people, dog-minded or not, would agree is basic common sense.

But one should also realize, when training is commenced, that if the training is going to be effective and successful, the trainer must first understand precisely with what kind of dog he is dealing. In other words, he must be able to judge his pupil and assess whether it possesses a bold, outgoing disposition or a quiet, gentle, retiring one. The first type needs holding back and restraint, i.e., more control enforced earlier, while the second almost certainly requires more encouragement, a gentler tone of voice, and most important, much praise for successfully accomplishing any exercise.

In short, one must realize that all dogs are different. They are as different in disposition and appearance as human beings. Appearance will vary even in a litter of all-black or all-yellow labrador pups, as an example. Every single one looks different to the person who understands dogs.

It is also essential to realize that, if punishment of any kind has to be administered, for it to be effective a dog must understand *why* it is being punished. Otherwise the whole unpleasant matter (for dog and handler) will have been in vain. For instance, take what is probably the most common problem of a dog's refusing to return to its owner when he calls it. The owner persists, getting more and more angry and frustrated as his commands are ignored. The dog is chased to no good effect and then eventually, in its own good time, returns apprehensively either to its owner or to its kennel. At this point the dog is seized, beaten, and scolded. Yet in the end no good at all has come of it. The whole episode has simply resulted in a terrified dog which is probably thinking that it has been beaten for returning home, since that was the last thing it did. In all instances, in fact, a dog can only relate punishment to the last thing that it did. And in this case it had in fact returned.

One's ability to judge when praise or correction should be given is one of the secrets to successful training. To the end of applying both in a timely and just manner, one should make an effort to think like a dog!

Due to its lack of reasoning powers as we understand them, a dog cannot, at least at first, interpret a command through its sense of hearing alone. It must be *shown* what action it must take in each exercise it is being taught if it is eventually to understand what you require of it. This again may seem like basic common sense, but certainly not so to the man who, on giving a simple command to a young and untrained dog which is not obeyed immediately, yells at it angrily and puts his boot into its ribs. Such action is comparable to that of a person who, unable to make a foreigner understand what he is saying, simply raises his voice!

As an example, when one is uttering the verbal command "Sit" to an untrained dog, the word itself means nothing. It is therefore necessary, in conjunction with giving the command, to *show* the dog what you require of it by pushing down on its haunches until it adopts the sitting position. At this point praise should be given both verbally and by way of a pat. Only in time, when the response you require has been linked by the dog to the verbal command, will it react to hearing alone.

The actual word one uses to obtain this or any other predictable response is irrelevant, provided the word relates to one action only and the dog is simultaneously shown the proper response. Repetition is therefore necessary until the dog eventually relates the spoken command alone to the action.

Voice tone is of major importance also, and a deliberate effort should be made to give commands firmly and quietly and to vary the tone with each separate command as one would (or should) do when giving praise or reprimanding. In addition, commands once given should not be repeated if the dog complies. I have in mind those people who persistently and monotonously urge their dog to "hunt 'em out" when the dog has been for a considerable time doing precisely that. Repeated commands are usually ignored and therefore ineffective, as the dog will get accustomed to the monotony of your voice in the background and simply "switch off."

Successful training depends to a large extent also upon self-control on the part of the trainer. Control of one's temper is of paramount importance. Training should be deferred whenever there is a risk that your irritation (even by something unrelated to your animal) may affect your good judgment where punishment for wrongdoing is concerned. Chastising a dog should never result from your loss of temper, irritating though your dog's disobedience may have been. Any response on his part to comply and perform correctly should be instantly rewarded with praise reinforced by your voice tone and attitude. It follows that temper control must be maintained in order that voice control, in turn, can instantly signal pleasure or displeasure towards the pupil.

Punishment should be short and sharp. I do not believe in beating a dog. My own method, if the circumstances warrant it, is to pick up the dog by the loose skin at the sides of the neck and shake it, while at the same time staring directly into its eyes and verbally chastising it. This I think can be far more effective than a beating. A bitch will dominate her puppy by gently holding it down by the throat, and adult dogs when fighting will endeavor to prevail by employing similar tactics. Dominance in the canine world is enforced in this way and this method of administering punishment is, as you can see, along similar lines.

An elderly gun-dog trainer I knew when I was a boy in England used to *growl* most realistically at a young dog that was getting out of line. The reaction of most dogs to this ploy was one of shocked amazement. He seemed to know how to do it just right, but as I do not, I cannot give any useful tips. It certainly worked for him!

Correction should also be enforced at the place where the offense was committed. For instance, in the case of the dog's failure to return when called, a thirty-foot check line should be attached to his collar and he should be allowed to drag it around freely. If, when called, the dog refuses to comply with the command, the line should be immediately stepped on and the dog brought to a sudden halt. He should then be quickly dragged back to where he was at the time he first failed to comply with the command, then shaken while the recall command is repeated loudly several times, in conjunction with the whistle signal if you are using a whistle at this stage. Associating correction with the *place* as well as enforcing it at the *time* it occurs makes for more effective learning.

In the same way, when you have ordered your dog to "stay," if he gets up and walks away he should immediately be taken back to where you had left him and be corrected there.

There are of course times when punishment cannot be given effectively because of a delay between the time the dog disobeyed and the time you are next in control of him. In this case it is best to hold off and leave matters alone as more harm than good will result if the dog is punished late. Let the incident go for the present and be prepared for the next time, when you can react in a timely way.

It is advisable, accordingly, to place yourself in such a position that you can ensure that your dog complies each time you give a command. Make a conscious effort not to keep shouting a command if the dog is disobeying and out of control. Keep quiet until you once more have him to hand, then try again.

Perhaps the most important advice I can give is this: Be sparing with any punishment you give and before resorting to it be absolutely sure you know your dog. Do not assume that punishment of the type I have described is necessary for every small slipup. Certain dogs need such correction if circumstances warrant it, but others of a milder and more sensitve disposition may never need anything harsher than a raised finger combined with a gruff "No." This simple admonishment is one of the first any pup should learn and it is more easily taught when he is young than at any other time.

Extra care should be exercised with puppies under six months of age. Roughness of any kind should never be resorted to with them. A more sensitive-natured animal can quickly and easily be ruined by unnecessarily harsh treatment. Encouragement and kindness are the passwords to success with this type of dog.

In sum, your approach where the administering of punishment is concerned should be appropriate to the individual dog. Being able to "read" your dog is a skill you should endeavor to master thoroughly before embarking on the first stages of actual training.

LIST OF COMMANDS

The words of command I generally use are as follows, but others may be used if preferred just as long as they are clearly understandable.

Walking to heel. Command "Heel." Point to left heel.

The recall. Call dog's name, command "Here," and/or give several pips on the whistle.

Sit and down. (This is best left until later in training.) Command "Sit." Raise right hand. Command "Down." Point to the ground.

Staunchness on point. Command "Whoa."

Retrieving. Command "Fetch." Give hand signal.

To hand over a bird. Command "Leave."

To ignore departure of a missed bird. Command "Gone away."

To cease disobedience. Command "No." (Shake dog if necessary.)

Casting off to hunt. Command "Get on." Snap the fingers.

To turn and keep close while hunting. Command "Come 'round" or give mouth whistle or two pips of plastic whistle. Give appropriate hand signal to cross to left or right.

FIRST POINTS

Naturally you will want to know whether your new puppy points. In order to determine this, there is no reason why you should not check things out even if he is only two or three months old. Some pups will exhibit pointing ability when even younger, as the desire to point should be instinctive and natural.

You may use one or more techniques to find out what he will do, the first being the old and well-proven method of using a game-bird wing attached to a fishing line on a pole. This wing-on-a-string method is to excite interest in order to see if the desire to point is in fact there.

A bird wing, which can be that of a quail, a pheasant, a duck, or a pigeon, as examples, is attached to the end of a fishing line; then, allowing for sufficient length of line, the fishing pole is held at such an angle that the wing just touches the ground. When the puppy is running loose, the wing is jigged around slightly while he's looking in the right direction. This will certainly arouse the pup's interest; he will probably stop, look, then dash in to try to grab it. But make quite sure he doesn't get his mouth on it. Do this by whipping the wing up and away in time; this is important.

Repeat the procedure, jigging the wing around in as tantalizing a way as possible. The slighter the movements, the more they will interest him and hold his attention. By now, having run at it several times and been unable to catch it, he should start to crouch and stalk the wing, exercising as much caution as he can so as not to scare the "bird" off again. In other words, he is pointing—pointing being nothing more than a stealthy stalk before the pounce (and kill) in the wild.

Pay very close attention to the pup's actions so that you can anticipate if he's going to pounce again. If he does, whip the wing away fast. If he points, do this only two or three times, then leave it alone for the day; otherwise he'll start getting bored and may then ignore the lure. A puppy's concentration span, like a child's, is very short indeed.

Resist the temptation to do this exercise more than another two or three times. It's only a game and a way of checking out the degree of pointing instinct; in my opinion it is worth nothing more than that. So you may now detach the wing and use the fishing equipment for its legitimate purpose.

Now it may well be that your pup won't stand and point the wing no matter what you do. If so, don't panic. Some pups will not take the slightest interest in this but will still turn out to be good pointers. Don't be overinfluenced by the results of the wing test alone. There is no reason at all why you shouldn't try the pup on live quail or pigeon.

If you do decide to use live birds, you must be sure to have the pup on a long leash or check line so that you can prevent any attempt to run in to try to catch the bird. If you are using quail, plant them by taking hold of each bird separately (two or three will do). Choose some suitable grass cover, not too deep, and release each bird directly into the grass. Do not let go of it a foot or two above the cover, as it will probably fly away and land elsewhere.

Remember exactly where the birds are, then bring the pup in towards them on the line from a downwind direction. This may assist him to locate them more easily as they will probably have moved around a little, thereby creating more scent. I say *may* assist him simply because at first, with many pups, scent in itself does not mean anything. Yet to some it instinctively does. With those which at first do not react to it, this will come later once they have had the opportunity to "sight-point" a few birds, which in turn teaches them to connect the scent with the bird itself. Because of this it may be necessary, for the pup to become really interested, that the quail move about in the grass ahead of him.

At this stage in all probability the stalking instinct will be aroused and he'll begin to stop and point, even though he has perhaps only seen the grass moving.

It is very important that you concentrate on the pup while this is taking place to ensure that he doesn't make a grab for the bird. Shorten the line and be ready to check him as he may by this time be eyeball to eyeball with it. If you can see that he is right on top of the bird, try to hold him back off it so that if it flushes it doesn't do so right under his nose and scare him. Make him hold the point for a short while if you can, and remember, the word "whoa" is of no avail at this stage as he doesn't yet know what it means. No purpose is served by using any command with a dog unless he has first been taught its meaning.

When the bird or birds flush and fly off, "mark" them well (watch where they land), as they probably won't go far. Then follow them up again applying the same tactics; that is, approaching from downwind.

After your pup has had a couple more successful points, leave it at that. Never overdo anything where pups are concerned.

If you decide to use a pigeon or two instead, plant them by placing the head beneath the wing, then tuck them into some suitably short cover. As an alternative—and for a puppy this is perhaps advisable—place the pigeon in a release cage, even though the object is not to release the bird from the trap as you will do later in training. You are using it merely to keep the bird in a specific place to reduce the possibility of its flying away too soon. Unlike quail which, once flushed, land fairly soon again, pigeon do not—they just keep going.

As with quail two or three successful points are sufficient, but do remember, between points, to move the cage and bird to a different location. It need not be far away; the object is to have

Blitz, an overeager young shorthair. He breaks point but the check line ensures he can't catch the bird.

Now he's beginning to learn. A nice point. Note the slack check line.

your puppy use his nose rather than his memory.

If you do decide to just plant the bird instead of using a release cage, be sure to hold the pup off when he is pointing it, so that if it flushes he will not be scared. A crack in the face from a wing can be very disconcerting to him.

By now you should have found out that your pup will point after all, so that's one less thing you have to worry about. You may leave matters at that for the moment as nothing will be spoiled by doing so. If on the other hand he really hasn't shown any point at all but nevertheless exhibits intense interest in birds, try him again when he is a week or two older; he may react better then. He could be a slow developer.

Should lack of desire to point persist after another month or two, however, it would be advisable to talk with a professional trainer. If he could take a look at your pup and perhaps try it out, this might well allay any fears or worries you have.

It would be nice to be able to walk out into the fields to test out pointing abilities on a few wild birds, but the chances of this are very limited unless you happen to reside near a well-stocked shooting preserve. For this reason, and since most training is conducted during the closed season, it is necessary to use pen-reared birds whether they be quail, chukar, pigeons, or pheasant. If sufficient birds are to be used to assure good training, there simply is no alternative. And in this respect don't let anyone convince you that pen-reared birds aren't any good. Actually they are a great aid to training and enable you to obtain the best results.

But more of that later. There is a lot of work to be done on your dog before serious training on birds commences.

THE LEASH AND WALKING TO HEEL

A question often posed by owners of puppies is, when can I start walking him on the leash? I recommend anytime from around ten to fourteen weeks.

A light leash and chain or just a nylon slip-cord leash should be used and the sooner your pup realizes that the leash means going out, and therefore something he enjoys, the sooner he will accept it. Let the pup drag the leash around for a while at first;

This one has him puzzled!

Lady, an English setter pup. Note the correct way to put on the choke chain.

If allowed to drag the leash around for a while, a pup will soon accept it.

in this way he will soon get used to its being around his neck. At this stage this is preferable to your holding the other end, since if you were to do so he would tend to fight and pull against it in a determined effort to slip out. With pups of timid disposition this can easily upset them. Better that he be allowed to drag it, as all he will do then is keep turning around and sniffing at it or roll over and play with it; he may even pick it up and carry it. Just walk on and allow him to do whatever he wishes, as he'll soon get bored and ignore the leash. At this point, he has accepted it.

You may now pick up the leash and walk alongside him holding onto it. He will of course pull as you walk along but now he will do so ahead of you and with more confidence. You may then start to pull back on the leash while giving the command "Heel" at the same moment. Try to make him walk along on your left with the leash across your front, held in your right hand. Your left hand is then free to pat him. When he's alongside you with the leash hanging loose he's walking correctly. Pups catch on to this more quickly than do older dogs.

As he complies with your "Heel" command and walks alongside you, say "Good boy!" and give him a pat as you walk on, repeating the corrective pull only when necessary. Only say "Heel" once when required and remember as you do so to pull him back in close. Don't keep on saying it as you walk along—it is not necessary if he's walking correctly and, even if you did, he would soon "switch off" and ignore you. Commands should be given (a) as infrequently as possible, (b) in a quiet but firm tone, and (c) without repetition unless he disobeys. In other words, if he's doing as he should be, keep quiet; speak only when he isn't.

When walking along, turn frequently to left and right rather than steering a straight course. Sudden turns will keep him guessing and help keep his attention focused on you.

With young potential gun dogs, I don't recommend strict parade-ground heel work off the leash until they have learned to hunt and quarter properly. This sometimes tends to make them "sticky"; in other words, confuse them and spoil their pattern when you're teaching quartering later. However, for pointing breeds, I do think that some heel work off the leash should be done before hunting is commenced as it helps with control later, especially if you have a dog that really wants to get out and run bigger than you would wish.

Once the pup is walking to heel correctly at all times on the

Ready to start heel-work training.

Muppy, a wirehaired pointing griffon, walking nicely to heel.

leash without pulling, you can begin to think about off-leash heel work with him. You should commence this by going back to square one again: dropping the leash and letting him trail it along while you go through the procedure of left and right and about turns. Have two or three sessions of this with the leash trailing, then during one of these sessions unclip the leash and just leave the choke chain on. If, however, it is a nylon slip-leash you are working with, tie it around his neck so that it is no longer trailing on the ground. The fact that he can still feel something around his neck, even though nothing is trailing, should influence him to stay alongside.

Go through the left and right turns and see that he complies, resorting to the use of the leash again only if he does not. Provided everything goes well, next time out try removing the chain (or the nylon leash), too; there is no reason why he should not conform and walk correctly alongside you. If he won't, then you have moved ahead too far, too quickly, and will have to go back a stage or two. The object of the exercise, in the end, is to make him understand that whenever you say "Heel" you want him to come on in and walk alongside you. But as with all other stages in training, you can only advance once the previous exercise has been thoroughly learned.

THE RECALL

Most young puppies will come to you readily when called or when you clap your hands—at least for a while. But later on other things, especially things that move, attract their interest and you are ignored. This is simply because the recall has not yet been instilled and is consequently not understood by the pup.

This can be irritating and at times has to be countered by adopting somewhat unorthodox methods. Ingenuity is the name of the game and what will work for one pup may not for the next, so you have to give the matter some thought in order to come up with a solution. In the meantime one should bear in mind two golden rules where the teaching of the recall is concerned: (1) Do not call your dog unless you can be sure you can make him comply. (2) Do not chase your dog, thereby allowing him to take the lead and thus the initiative; always try to have *him* come to *you*.

The following maneuvers usually do the trick with most pups.

First, call his name in conjunction with the recall command "Here" and, if this fails, run away from him the moment you have his attention. From the very beginning, use the whistle with the recall command, giving several pips. This will eventually be the signal in the field to call him to you from a distance, so the sooner he is trained to it the better. The whistle is a good attention-getter and is often reacted to far better than the voice. As you are by now moving away from him, the chances are good that he will follow you, as anything that is moving (yourself included) is of far more interest to a pup than whatever is standing still.

If he continues to pay less attention to you than he should, call his name and give the whistle signal, then quickly conceal yourself. Sooner or later he will notice you are missing and will probably become concerned and start looking for you. As soon as he does, call and whistle again and give him lots of praise when he gets to you. However, I must also point out that this approach is normally effective only when used in an area that he is unfamiliar with. This circumstance in itself will cause most pups to pay more attention to your whereabouts.

You may have noticed that the recall command "Here" sounds virtually the same as the command "Heel." This is appropriate as one complements the other. The only way any dog can walk alongside you at heel is to come in to you from wherever he is. You are therefore using the two commands for virtually the same purpose.

There are times when problems with the recall can be counteracted by giving the miscreant a cookie or some of his favorite dog meal. Food temptation is hard to resist for most pups, who will willingly respond if such a treat is in the offing. However, I advise that bribery be used only as a last resort. Any well-balanced puppy or adult dog, if started right, should return to you eagerly when called without the incentive of food. Praise is all that should be necessary.

If disobedience persists, though, there is usually no alternative but to resort to the use of a check line and choke chain. A line about fifteen to twenty feet long will do. Put on the choke chain attached to the line and let him trail it along as he runs ahead of you in the field. The presence of the line should not trouble him as he has probably become accustomed to the feel of the leash trailing. As he is running around, shout "Here" and give the whistle signal too; if he fails to comply, slam your foot down on the line and bowl him head over heels. At this point, grab hold of the line, repeat the command and the whistle signal, and at the very same moment give a sharp, hard tug on the line. He should now come running in towards you. As he does, give several more pips on the whistle, and lots of praise when he gets to you.

When he starts to run towards you remember not to pull on the line again. Don't drag him towards you under any circumstances; he must learn to run back freely. Repeat this another two or three times, then leave it for the day. More often would be counterproductive as he would then be reluctant to get very far away from you.

Over the next two or three weeks have a few more sessions, going about it in exactly the same way. Then, when it seems to be taking effect, remove the line and substitute for it the short leash. He'll be able to tell the difference all right as there will be less drag from the leash, but he'll still think you possess that mysterious ability to control him from a distance. After a further two or three sessions, provided all has gone well, try removing the leash altogether while leaving the choke chain on. This will still provide a "link" (in more than one sense) between you and him. The chances are good that by this time you will find you have won and that shortly you will not need to put the choke chain on at all. Try to discontinue the use of the line as soon as possible, once he will come to you without hesitation.

It is clear that, if a puppy is taught the recall correctly early in life, returning to you becomes second nature. So if problems persist, there is something you aren't doing right. You must sit down and try to analyze where you are going wrong.

INTRODUCTION TO THE GUN

It is probably correct to say that the two most common problems caused by owners of young potential gun dogs are retrieving faults and gun nervousness.

Introduction of a puppy to the sound of gunfire is a matter to which unfortunately too little thought is given by many people. Thus, due to the methods they employ, the seeds of gun nervousness are often sown, the first stages of which can be difficult for the inexperienced to detect. If the owner continues to plow ahead, matters worsen until serious problems have developed, which in turn prevent normal progress in all other aspects of training the dog for the field.

In using the term "gun nervousness" I do not mean "gun shyness." The two are usually quite different and affect a dog for different reasons, as will be explained in chapter 6.

Starting to get a puppy accustomed to the sound of a gun being discharged is a most critical stage in its education. Done incorrectly and thoughtlessly it can result in problems which are difficult if not impossible to cure. Introduced correctly, however, gunfire should cause no fear and will be regarded by a pup as an everyday occurrence.

The owner of a labrador which was brought to me solely because of this problem admitted that he had introduced the dog as a puppy to the sound of gunfire by firing .38 blanks inside his home, where the pup lived. The dog became a nervous wreck and proved incurable. I did not inquire as to the state of his wife's nerves, but I do know that, had I been resident there, mine would have been as bad as the dog's! This is an extreme example but it illustrates my point about being more thoughtful and trying to look at the matter from the dog's point of view.

Gunfire should be introduced gradually and unobtrusively while a young dog is engaged in some activity which it enjoys. Its mind is then occupied with other things when the shot is fired; consequently the sound is less likely to startle it. There are several ways of doing this, of which I shall describe only my favorite method as a I believe it to be the best.

The time I choose is when the pup is running free ahead of me in the fields; personally, I can't think of any activity a dog enjoys more. I take with me a .22-blank pistol and, while the pup is running well ahead, I fire a shot with the pistol behind my back. He may stop, turn, and look at me or he may ignore it altogether, but whichever he does, I just walk on as though the sound is one of the most natural things in the world. When the opportunity presents itself again, I fire once more. A puppy of the right temperament is not troubled by it in the slightest.

Proceeding in the manner I have described, and provided your puppy is unconcerned, you can then wait until he's a little closer and fire again, still with the pistol behind your back. Do this four or five times during a fifteen-minute run, then leave it until the next time you are out. Continue the process each time you exercise him while watching his reaction carefully to ensure that the gunfire is not troubling him.

Heidi, a German shorthaired pointer, running freely ahead while occasional shots are fired.

When you are perfectly satisfied that he's not in the least worried about the sound of the blank pistol, you may try firing a .410 shotgun. It should be discharged at a distance at first, preferably by another member of the family. You can then progress, if everything continues to go well, to the twelve-gauge. As likely as not, probably within two weeks or so, you will have successfully gotten over this important hurdle in your puppy's education.

However, we must also consider the possibility that things may not go right. If signs of fear or nervousness appear, such as the pup's walking or running back to you with its tail down, stop immediately and proceed as recommended in chapter 6.

INTRODUCTION TO WATER

Many of the pointing breeds are not as enthusiastic about water as spaniels and retrievers. In fact, some of them downright detest it. However, there are people who own German shorthairs, for example, who will want their dog to swim out and retrieve from water. They may intend to use the dog for duck hunting as well as upland hunting and there is no reason not to do so if the weather isn't too severe. A lot of GSPs make good water dogs.

There are those owners, though, who will have no intention of using their dog for water work, and what follows will be of little or no interest to them. For those who are interested, however, I shall describe the best way of introducing a puppy to water so that he will enjoy it. Indeed, that he enjoy it right from the start is important if you want him to be enthusiastic about the water later on.

Always try to take a puppy to the water during the summer months when the water is warm. If your pup happens to be from a late fall or early winter litter, wait until the weather is suitable before doing anything. Like his owner, a pup is going to enter warm water more willingly.

Choose a spot where the bank shelves down gradually and walk right to the water's edge with him. He may sniff at it cautiously at first, then venture in slowly and paddle around for a while, taking great care not to get out of his depth. If he seems reluctant to go in any further, try wading in with him in an effort to get him to swim. This approach can work effectively.

Pups of the same age in a group can be a great source of encouragement to one another. Some will enter and swim readily while others will hold back and plod about in the shallows, reluctant to take the plunge. Usually, though, during all the hustle and bustle and chasing around, and without realizing what they have done, they're very soon in and having the time of their lives.

If you have only one pup, an older dog belonging to a friend can often be of great help. Allowing the older dog to swim out and around encourages the pup to do likewise.

If necessary, try wading in again yourself but further out this time, carrying the pup with you. Place him gently in the water, let him go, and rest assured he'll swim all right— they all can. He may be a little scared at first, but with praise and encouragement he will quickly get to like it.

If he is an enthusiastic retriever of the dummy, try encouraging him by using that. At first just drop it on the very edge of the water, allowing him to grasp it while getting only his front legs wet. Next time drop it a few inches further out, and so on, gradually increasing the distance until finally he can't resist pushing out and swimming for it. This will only work though with a pup that loves to retrieve. Indeed, I have known some which were uninterested in picking up and carrying on land at first but would swim out and fetch with great enthusiasm in water. With this type of pup, teaching water retrieving first will sometimes encourage land retrieving later.

All else failing—and I do this only as a last resort when they are at least four or five months old—I attach a long check line to the collar and wade into the creek. If calling the pup first has failed, having reached the opposite bank I gently pull him into the water. When he enters it, the line is immediately relaxed as he starts to swim across, and lots of praise and encouragement is given. If it is done several times, first in one direction, then in the other, this procedure usually does the trick. Before very long he'll enter willingly, without the persuasion of the line, and swim across to you. Few dogs require this expedient, however, and only occasionally have I had to resort to it.

I am adamantly against a reluctant swimmer's being thrown bodily into the water. Such tactics usually result from loss of temper and are completely unnecessary. As with all other aspects of training, patience, consistency, and thoughtfulness are the secrets of success.

Initial Training

OBSERVATIONS ON STEADINESS

The question of whether a gun dog needs to steady to wing and shot is a matter often discussed when sportsmen get together. And the decision on whether to train a dog oneself or have the dog trained by someone else to this standard usually depends upon a variety of factors.

A steady gun dog is one which will remain staunch on point and stay there perfectly steady (a) when the bird is flushed, (b) when it is shot, and (c) until commanded to retrieve. Any dog trained to do this is a truly finished and polished gun dog and one to be proud of in any company, yet relatively few come up to this criterion. Most simply run in prior to the shot in the expectation of a retrieve once the bird is flushed.

Attaining steadiness in any gun dog takes considerable time, and this applies whether it is the owner or a professional who is doing the training. It is a slow, repetitive process and there are no shortcuts to success.

Many hunters prefer that their dogs break and run in to retrieve without command as soon as a bird is flushed. Probably the dogs they owned and hunted before always did, so they see no need for a change—which is fine if that is preferred. The choice is up to the individual and if a man's dog does the job he asks of it, who can criticize him?

The standard to which you want your dog trained is therefore entirely a matter for you to decide. The necessary procedure for training him properly is set forth in this book. But however far you decide to go, provided that what training you do is carried out consistently, firmly, and with patience, you should finish up with a good, sound gun dog.

WHEN TO START

Opinions vary as to when one should commence serious training with a young gun dog, which of course entails from that time on a firmer approach to the instilling of discipline. A point to be borne in mind when considering this—and it is one I have mentioned earlier and make no apology for doing so again—is that every dog is different from the next. Some possess a bold and confident temperament while others are more sensitive. What one is able to do with any dog from, say, six months of age on therefore depends to a great extent upon its disposition. What you can achieve with one in a given length of time may not be possible with another of the same age. However, you should of course know by now precisely what type of dog you are dealing with.

I have found that with most gun-dog breeds, eight months of age or thereabouts is the time one can start more serious training. This is an age at which you are usually able to put on that little bit of extra pressure needed to assure steadiness right from the start.

I disagree with those who advocate strict training schedules for dogs. They will establish inflexible projected progress charts as though dealing with the fabrication of a piece of machinery. Training aims are laid down, categorically stating that, as of a certain date, the dog should be doing so and so. Dog training never has worked and never will work successfully that way. While you may be lucky with a particular dog and get away with it without too many problems cropping up, you have to remember that a dog isn't a machine. It can't be programmed like a computer. A dog is capable of thought, emotions, doubts, and fears—each in its own way. Since no two are alike, no single method will work for all.

The novice can very quickly get himself into serious problems if he is unable to recognize warning signs that the particular dog he's working with "can't take it." Unable to quickly detect the symptoms, this owner may, through frustration, continue to plow ahead, possibly forcing the dog into deep, deep trouble.

If you look upon your dog as an individual and train him at the pace best suited to his own ability, you will have far better results. You will then have a dog that has enjoyed his training, not one that was forced to endure it. Because of this you will have a better hunting companion in the end.

THE "WHOA" COMMAND AND STOPPING TO WHISTLE

The command "Whoa" (meaning to stop and stand) is as important to the pointing breeds as "Hup" (meaning sit and stay) is to flushing dogs. If you ever hope to have a pointing dog working under control and holding point staunchly, it is essential that the "whoa" command be thoroughly taught before the dog is allowed to work on birds.

Having located and while pointing a bird, a dog can be reminded by the command "Whoa" to remain still and hold the point and not move up closer, crowding the bird. If he is allowed to do the latter it will inevitably lead to a flush, maybe before the handler has had time to get in close enough to take a shot. It is a most useful command, also, in pheasant hunting when, for instance, a crafty old cock bird, preferring to run rather than fly, scuttles off with head down through the underbrush. The temptation can be strong for the dog to trail what is a very hot scent, usually at a far faster pace than the handler can keep up with. The "whoa" command can be of considerable assistance then also. A running pheasant, unless wounded, is unlikely to change his tactics suddenly and bury himself in cover. More likely than not, as soon as the dog gets too close on his tail, he

Teaching the "whoa" command. Note the short leash for the early stages of this exercise.

will take to wing, resulting in a lost opportunity if the dog isn't stoppable.

The "whoa" command can in fact be taught to a dog in two completely separate ways. First, of course, it must be taught as a verbal command; but it can be taught as a whistle command in addition. The verbal command is for such occasions as when the dog has gone on point and you are approaching. If he's holding staunch, of course it isn't necessary, but it will be if you detect any sign of movement on his part, at which time the command should be uttered *once* in a quiet, soothing, drawn-out manner. On the other hand, when the dog is hunting at a distance, a single blast on the whistle can be far more effective. Moreover, nothing disturbs wild game more than the human voice; not so a whistle.

If the verbal and whistle commands are taught simultaneously during training, each can be as effective as the other under particular circumstances. For the same reasons flushing dogs are taught to "hup" to both also.

To begin you will need, in addition to the whistle, the leash and choke chain. You have already got your dog accustomed to the leash and by now he should be walking along without pulling at your left, whether on or off it. Start by placing the leash and chain on the dog and do some heel work. After a few minutes of this, as you are walking along, in a quiet voice give the command "Whoa" and at the same time raise your right hand in front of the dog so that he can clearly see it. That visual signal is very important as you will realize later. As you are doing this, have the whistle ready in your mouth (no problem at all provided you have it on a lanyard around your neck) and, as you call the "whoa" command, give a single pip on the whistle—that's all. For the first session or two he may not react as you would like him to. He may walk on or pull back with surprise or even sit down. If any of these things happen, just stand him up again alongside you and repeat the command.

If he does react correctly the first time, pat and praise him. Remain there for at least twenty seconds while he stands alongside and say nothing more. Never repeat a command if the dog has complied. After the pause, say "Heel," walk on again for twenty or thirty yards, and repeat the process. Remember to set him up alongside you if necessary and to praise him if he complies. Don't overdo the praise; just a "Good boy!" and a pat are sufficient. And remember that the verbal command and the whistle signal must come virtually together.

Continue doing this for a while, stopping and whoaing him as many as twenty times if necessary; if he's complying well, fewer commands will do. Then leave it at that for the day, the object at this stage simply being to have him stop when you tell him, remain standing alongside, and move off with you again when you say "Heel." This exercise can become boring but it is essential yard training and vitally important if you are to end up with a well-disciplined gun dog.

The next time out and for several more sessions, do the same again, preferably in the same area each time. When you feel that your dog is beginning to get the idea, and you will know this by noting that he is stopping automatically as you do, start to give only one or the other command: sometimes the verbal "Whoa," sometimes one pip on the whistle. By now he should be reacting well to either. Continue this each time you go out until you are satisfied that he will comply without fail. When training, you must always avoid stepping up to the next rung on the ladder until the animal has thoroughly mastered the current one.

At the end of each training session, provided everything has gone as you wanted it to, allow the dog to relax by playing with him and giving him a run. This will break the tension and add to his enjoyment in going out with you.

The next stage is to teach your dog to remain standing where you stopped him while you move away. This also has to be taken a step at a time. Walk him to heel again but this time with the leash dragging along the ground. "Whoa" him verbally and by the whistle and then, while he's standing there, give him the verbal reminder and the hand signal again. Now slowly back away and to the front of him for a yard or two. He may move, but if you have done the groundwork well he'll probably stay right there. If he does move, remember the rule always to put the dog right back where he originally was. Never let him get away with anything without correction. Repeat the command and the hand signal and step away again. Stand in front of him for a few seconds, saying nothing if he stays, then walk back to your original position alongside him and tell him he's a good dog. Whatever you do at this stage, don't call him to you once you have told him to "whoa." He must interpret that for the moment to mean he should stand there until you return.

If all is going well after two or three times of moving a yard or two away from him, try moving away further and walk to left and right in front of him. But be ready to react instantly when he shows any sign of moving. If you watch your dog closely you'll be able to tell what he's going to do before he does it! In time, and fairly soon at that, you should be able to start walking right around the dog while he stands there good and steady. It is at this stage that you may consider removing the leash. But leave the choke chain on for the time being.

If you find you are having problems, and you are thinking of putting on the long check line due to unsteadiness as you gradually increase your distance from him, you will have to go back a stage or two for reinforcement. Contrary to what you may have thought, you haven't got through to him well enough yet or he would stay in place. You may well need to use the check line later when whoaing him during the early stages of quartering, but even then it should be avoided if at all possible.

When he's complying, test him by pulling *gently* on the leash after having given the command, "whoa."

One good test to see if your dog has grasped the "whoa" command exercise properly is to step back while holding on to the leash and, having given him a reminder by voice or hand signal, gently pull on the leash. He should stand there and resist; if he does, increase the pull slightly so that he is leaning against it. You can even have someone else do this, but if you do, be sure that person understands not to pull the dog too hard. Just a steady and firm but moderate pull to test his determination to stay is sufficient.

By now you should be able to remove the choke chain too and you are ready to start the second stage which entails walking away from him perhaps twenty-five yards, calling him to you, and stopping him en route. But before we go any further, let me say this: You may at first find a reluctance on the dog's part to move and come to you. This is perfectly natural and as it should be. After all, until now he has always been required to stay exactly where you whoaed him until you returned. Now you are not returning to him but are asking him to come to you, so this is bound to raise doubts in his mind for a while. Have patience though and he will soon (albeit with hesitation) begin to walk towards you. Remember to use both the verbal and whistle commands (several pips) and do not attempt for the moment to "whoa" him as he approaches you. This must be left for the first session or two until he gets accustomed to the game of first staying and then running to you when called.

Do not be tempted to call him to you every time you walk away. Return to him from time to time. If you called him each time he might soon form the opinion that you would always do so, and you would eventually turn around to find him already on his way towards you. You must change things around so that he will not try to anticipate you.

No matter how far away from him you walk (and this you should vary), on stopping and turning to face the dog never call him to you immediately. Always wait for a while as he stands and watches you. The reason for this is quite simple. Dogs are in general very attentive; most watch your movements very carefully, although you may not have realized it; hence the value of hand signals when working a dog. Every movement you make transmits a message, whether you are getting your car keys from your pocket or your gun from its case. The dog soon comes to recognize what each action means.

If, therefore, you get into the habit of calling the dog to you at the very moment you have stopped and turned, he will interpret the stopping and turning as the signal to leave without waiting for the command. Looked at from his point of view, this is perfectly logical. So remember, once you have stopped and turned, stand and wait. How long is up to you but, as with the distance, try to vary it. The reason for this is simply that the period of time you wait before giving him the command to come (here) is the key to keeping him standing and waiting. It helps make him remember that only your voice or the whistle—nothing else—is the signal allowing him to move.

When he is running readily to you on command, you may start to "whoa" him as he approaches you. After calling and whistling him, and when he is about half way to you, suddenly raise your right hand high, give the command "Whoa," and pip the whistle all at the same time. He may stop suddenly in his tracks just as you had hoped he would, but compliance the first time doesn't always mean too much—he may have just reacted out of sheer surprise!

If he doesn't stop but instead just slows down as he wanders towards you, get hold of him and take him back to where he was at the time you ordered him to "whoa." Set him up there again, repeat the "whoa" command, and walk back to where you were. Wait a short time, call him on again, and try a second time. This time it should work. In fact, it would have worked from the first if you had done everything properly.

Remember always to give praise when deserved but do not overdo it. Some dogs will get overexcited and think it is playtime; but a quiet "Good boy!" is always appreciated.

If he is now whoaing correctly when half way to you, you may extend your distance somewhat and try stopping him twice on the way in. In other words, walk out, turn, stand and wait, call "Here," then stop him with the usual signals. Stand and wait a short while again, then call him and stop him a second time before concluding by calling him all the way in to you.

At this stage it can be most useful to go through all you have done so far. This little test is always worthwhile as this part of any dog's training is so very important. Walk him to heel on the leash and stop and "whoa" him several times; then remove the leash and do the same again. Next, having told him "Whoa," go through the exercise of walking away and around him, remembering to walk back to him now and then to praise him for staying. Conclude by walking off some distance, calling him up, and whoaing him several times while he's on the way towards you.

It is repetition, I know, but if you go through all this and your dog does consistently well, you're making good progress.

Next, we will take up whoaing him when he is actually hunting, while he is being taught to quarter.

QUARTERING

The purpose of hunting any gun dog is so that it will use its nose in order to locate, point, and subsequently retrieve game that is shot. In doing so it should quarter ahead of and to each side of its handler so as to thoroughly cover the ground within a range compatible with cover conditions.

A gun dog not doing this is not working to the best possible advantage.

Range in relation to hunting cannot be misinterpreted where the flushing breeds are concerned. They must hunt at all times within shooting distance; otherwise birds flushed are going to be unshootable. Therefore there can be no argument about range as it relates to these breeds.

However, in this book we are concerned solely with pointing breeds, and the distance at which any individual dog of such a breed will work can vary greatly. And herein lies the controversy about which I can give no better advice than that already outlined in the section on "Choice of Breed" in chapter 1.

We have to presume therefore that you did your homework thoroughly and that you have chosen a dog which does in fact tend to keep fairly close contact—at least so far! This may well change later once he begins to really understand what birds are; but for the moment, he does not.

Obviously, people's views regarding range in pointing dogs are going to vary a lot, mainly depending upon where and under what conditions a dog is being hunted. My own idea of a comfortable distance connotes a dog that will hunt and quarter within a range of approximately sixty to eighty yards on either side of its handler and about thirty to forty yards ahead, at the maximum. Some pointing-dog purists will disagree with this and say that they want their dog to get out much further. Well, if they do then that's fine. Whatever a man is happy with in his own dog is what matters. He after all is hunting it and he more than anyone else must be satisfied with its performance.

However, as far as the average hunting man is concerned, I am convinced he wants a dog to work within the limits I have outlined and, in fact, closer than that when hunting in woods, especially before the leaves have fallen.

The object of the next exercise, therefore, is to teach your dog to do just that and, as I stated earlier in this book ("Humanizing," chapter 1), this process should have commenced right at the beginning by your not allowing your puppy to run way out while exercising him in the fields. Keeping close means keeping close *at all times*, not just when hunting.

It may well prove necessary to use the check line with some dogs while teaching this, at least for a while, but if you find your dog reacts well without it, then avoid doing so. Far better that he be taught without its use if at all possible. We must presume though, for the moment, that its use is preferred, so place the choke chain on the dog and clip the line to it. Take the dog out onto a flat, open field with low cover and cast him off to hunt, using the appropriate command "Get on," and work him into the wind. This will help with his pattern, and any prospective gun dog from good "working breeding" will hunt without the incentive of birds being there.

Try to maintain as straight a course as you can while your dog is hunting. *He's* supposed to be doing the quartering, not you. However, it may prove necessary, if your dog's pattern is erratic or if he is boring out ahead too far, for you to walk in a weaving or zig zag manner in an effort to get him to hunt across your front to left and right. In other words, as he is off to your left, you should walk out to your right slightly, at the same time giving the whistle signal (two pips) to turn him. Then, as you gain his attention, give the appropriate arm signal to get him back

Teaching quartering. Muppy, taking signals nicely, first crosses to handler's left . . .

. . . then to the right . . .

. . . then back across to the left again. This exercise helps ensure a good pattern when hunting.

At greater speed, Sprite, an English setter, hunts ahead . . .

. . . maintaining a nice pattern . . .

. . . under control and at an ideal working distance.

across the front of you and vice versa. Try to straighten out your own course again though as soon as he begins to get the idea.

Make every effort to keep him within the distance I have recommended and enforce this if necessary by following him up and stepping on the line at the precise time you give the two pips on the whistle. This will stop him or even bowl him over suddenly. Two or three times of this and he will begin to listen better.

Be sure also to use a verbal command in conjunction with the whistle. I say "Come 'round." After using them both together for a while, you can vary things by using one or the other. The reason for this is that one day you may forget to take your whistle along.

Practice this for session after session until your dog will quarter in a nice even pattern from side to side ahead of you, while turning instantly in response to the two whistle pips and your verbal command "Come 'round" when at the furthest limit of each cast. Only by repeatedly stopping him with the check line, and shaking him up too if necessary, will you succeed in correcting disobedience where this exercise is concerned.

You should also take the opportunity while doing this to occasionally "whoa" him. At first you should try it only when he is passing across fairly close to you, then as he gets the idea you can gradually increase the distance at which you give the command. All that's required is a sudden raising of the right arm, the command "Whoa," and the single whistle pip—all together. If he stops as he should, have him stand there a few seconds, then cast him off to hunt again. This can be done from where you are standing.

If he doesn't stop as he should, you know the procedure by now: Get right out there, catch hold of him, and take him back to where he was at the time you gave the command. Stand him while repeating the commands, then leave him there and walk back to where you were. Pause a short time, then cast him off again.

Assuming you taught the "whoa" command well originally, he'll soon get the idea. Just have patience.

Once he has developed a nice pattern working into the wind you must hunt him downwind too; that is, with the wind on your back. With experience any good dog will make use of wind direction while hunting and you will see this begin to develop as time goes on. For instance, as you may have noticed, a dog quartering into the wind will tend to maintain a fairly even pattern ahead of and to the left and right of you, cover conditions permitting of course. The same dog hunting downwind will tend to pull out ahead a little further than normal and hunt back into the wind towards you in an effort to get bird scent blown in towards him. On the other hand, a wind blowing in from your left will make a dog work deeper to your right and vice versa.

When you feel confident you can remove the check line, do so, but for the moment leave the choke chain on (that psychological link again!). He is less likely to start misbehaving if he can still sense its presence. But as soon as you can dispense with that also, you should.

I suggested that you teach quartering in fairly open country at first for a very specific reason; i.e., your dog's pattern will benefit and you will be in a better position to correct misbehavior than you would be in thicker cover. Having taught him this in somewhat easy conditions, though, you must then work him where it is not possible to maintain the same mechanical pattern, that is, in woodland. For the grouse and woodcock hunter especially this is essential, since this is where the birds are going to be when you are actually shooting over him.

Only start this though once he has learned to comply instantly with your whistle or verbal command to turn. The reason for this is that once he is doing this reliably, the check line will no longer be required. This will be far better for your own composure because I guarantee that, if used in woodland, it will entangle itself in everything within reach!

Obviously in woodland and thick underbrush, both you and your dog are going to have to make your way through as best you can. You will know when you are in there, in light of the prevailing conditions, how far from you he can be permitted to hunt. If you judge this on the basis of not letting him get out of your sight for more than a few seconds at a time, you won't go far wrong.

Incidentally, now that you are getting him accustomed to hunting in woodland, you can if you wish put a bell on his collar.

Most grouse and woodcock hunters place a small bell on their dog so that in dense cover conditions it will assist in locating the dog when he gets out of sight—which most of them do most of the time! The bell tinkles constantly while the dog is on the move and as long as it can be heard by the hunter, he knows his dog is not on point. However, when the sound of the bell suddenly ceases, he has probably located a bird. All that remains then is for the hunter to walk into the area where he last heard the bell and locate his dog.

In theory, of course, if a dog is always hunting within sight of its handler, a bell is unnecessary. But during most woodland hunting this is not the case. Obviously, the dog will at times be out-of-sight and nothing can be done to prevent this from happening even with the closest of workers. So I recommend the use of a bell by grouse and woodcock men. It is extremely useful.

RETRIEVING DUMMIES

It is fair to say that if a weakness is going to exist in any pointing dog—including those in the category of versatile pointing breeds, i.e., which hunt, point, and retrieve—then as likely as not retrieving is going to be it.

This is understandable as one always hopes that the dominant desire in a pointing dog will be to point, just as one always hopes that that in a labrador will be to retrieve. If either type lacks this specific instinctive trait, it is not worth training.

Retrieving in many of the pointing breeds is at best a doubtful quality, some doing so naturally and with enthusiasm whereas others (perhaps the larger percentage) exhibit little or no eagerness.

This situation is hardly surprising in the case of pointers and setters because for generations in the field-trial world retrieving has not been required of them. Any inherent trait in any line if unused or discouraged through selective breeding for several generations gradually wanes and may in time disappear altogether.

If retrieving is going to be required, therefore, it is well to start while the dog is as young as possible, especially if the desire to do so clearly exists, and we will at this stage assume that it does.

I am a firm believer in the use of a canvas retrieving dummy to teach a young dog to handle retrieves correctly and to deliver to hand nicely. Retrieving is far better taught with a dummy than by the use of dead birds, as correction can be enforced if required during dummy retrieving which might be inadvisable if a young dog were retrieving a bird. He might for instance associate any correction given with the bird itself, thereby possibly creating problems later on when pointing and staunchness training commences. In addition, the longer a pointing dog is prevented from picking up and carrying birds, the easier it will be to train him to be steady to wing and shot when you eventually start on it; his desire to chase will be that much less. I also recommend that the dummy be used without a bird wing attached, for the very same reasons.

When trying out your dog as a puppy to see if the interest in retrieving was present, all you did was throw the object and let him run to pick it up. Now things must change. He is at the stage where you can put to good use the "whoa" exercise by making him stand steady alongside you while you throw the dummy for him to fetch. You may not realize it, but in so doing you are in fact getting into the very first stages of steadiness to wing, albeit in an artificial manner. Yet if it is done thoroughly now, it will help immeasurably when you eventually begin teaching your dog to remain steady to flying birds.

In starting the retrieve exercise, be aware that at first your dog may break and run in after the dummy despite the fact that you have first given him the command "Whoa." The reason for this is quite simple. Previously, when told to "whoa," there was no temptation for him to move; now there is, so be prepared for him to break so that you can act quickly to correct him.

In order to counteract this possibility, this is one instance in which I do recommend using the check line or the long leather leash. Either will do. Clip it to the choke chain and allow the other end to trail along the ground so that you can stand on it. First give him the command "Whoa" with the hand signal, then throw the dummy and brace yourself! At that point he may well break and take off after it. If he does, don't yell at him. Say

Jason, a German shorthaired pointer, stays steady at heel.

The dummy is thrown, which Jason marks.

nothing. He's in for a big shock anyway when he hits the end of the line. Then just haul him back alongside you and tell him "Whoa" again. Step out in front of him while ensuring he stays there, walk out yourself, and pick up the dummy.

The object of picking up the dummy yourself is twofold: (1) You are demonstrating to him that a retrieve is a reward given only for doing right, and (2) you are teaching him good manners in making him stand and stay while you get the reward instead. From the very beginning he must learn that not all retrieves are his—only those that you tell him he can have. Good manners are essential if bracework, i.e., working with another well-trained dog, is to be undertaken later.

You should also start using the command "Gone away" now each time you walk out to pick up the dummy yourself. This simply tells the dog "no retrieve," the significance of which will become more apparent later when birds fly away unshot.

Having picked up the dummy, walk back to him with it and repeat the process, remembering to stand on the line again. Don't let him get away with a break if possible, but if he does, correct him again in exactly the same way. If on the other hand he remains steady, wait a while, twenty seconds at least, then give the command for him to fetch. And remember to get your foot off the line before you send him. If he gets bowled over after you have commanded him to retrieve, he will to say the least be somewhat puzzled!

Many pointer trainers, in addition to giving the command to retrieve, touch the dog lightly on top of the head. Teaching this "contact" command can be most useful in that it tells a dog to wait until he receives that tap on the head before moving. If you want to use this additional command you may do so, as long as you do it consistently. By this I mean that it will be necessary to use it each and every time you send the dog for a retrieve, whether in training or under actual hunting conditions. There will be times while hunting when this will present certain difficulties. However, the choice is yours.

If there is any sign of hesitation in bringing the dummy back to you once the dog has picked it up, give several pips on the whistle and call him in. But refrain from doing this if he will return with it swiftly without encouragement. It is far better if he can be relied upon to do so because under practical hunting conditions he may, for instance, be hunting for a shot bird in deep cover, out of sight. How then can you give him any signal to return with a bird you do not know he has found? Always try to have a willing retriever bring a dummy or bird in to you without being cajoled, even though with many dogs it simply isn't possible.

Make sure that he hands the dummy to you properly. Try to keep him from dropping it in front of you. Move back several paces if necessary to keep the dog coming on towards you, or turn away and gently take the dummy from him when he's alongside. Stroke and praise him while he still holds the dummy

A nice delivery to hand. As shown here, bird wings were later attached to the dummy. This often encourages an otherwise reluctant retriever.

in his mouth, then gently take it from him, saying "Leave." Your hands are the focus of his attention as he comes in towards you, since you are holding them out to receive the dummy. A dog which associates your hands with kindness and praise will approach them more willingly than one that associates them with punishment.

It is not necessary that he sit to hand over. A good retrieve is one in which a dog comes straight up to you proudly and makes a nice high-headed delivery right into your hand. Surprisingly, many people actively encourage or even order a dog to drop the bird in front of them. I think this is a very bad practice, especially when the dog would otherwise have quite happily delivered right to hand. A wounded pheasant, if dropped out of reach, will leg it off for the nearest cover and may consequently escape.

Any gun dog that retrieves well *naturally* is worth its weight in gold!

Go through the process again, still with the leash or line trailing, but without your standing on it if he has remained steady. If, on the other hand, you are still unsure how he will react, continue to stand on the line until you feel more confident of him. Just how well you instilled the "whoa" command will be revealed at this stage.

If all goes well for five or six throws, leave it for that day. And please note, I said *throws*, not *retrieves*, as you should always remember not to allow him to pick up all of them. Instead you must constantly make him wonder what you are going to do next, which in turn will result in his waiting until you reveal your intentions by your command. By waiting to hear what you have to say he will develop good manners and consequently steadiness, as one is so much a part of the other.

You may repeat this exercise two or three times the same week, giving him four or five retrieves to every six or seven throws. After a week or two of this, provided he's standing and staying well on the "whoa" command, remove the leash and chain and advance a little by walking away from him a few yards and throwing the dummy from where you stand. Pause for a reasonable length of time, then give the command to retrieve, unless of course you are also using the tap-on-the-head method. In this case you would walk back alongside the dog first.

You can gradually increase the distance you throw from provided all continues to go well. By way of further temptation, throw the dummy from time to time towards or past him so that it falls relatively close to where he is standing. If he is going to break at all, now is the time. If he holds, then you've done your yard work thoroughly and you can give yourself a pat on the back! If on the other hand unsteadiness persists, you haven't spent as much time as you should have on the basics, so leave the retrieve and go back and reinforce the earlier training. Unless basic control is thoroughly instilled you will never have a reliably steady and well-disciplined dog. And achieving reliability should be the object of each exercise.

Remember, the period of time you stand and wait, having thrown out the dummy, until the moment you give the command to retrieve is the key to steadiness success. To allow any dog to run in as the dummy hits the ground or, worse still, as it is descending, will guarantee an unsteady dog for evermore. He will take the sight of the dummy falling and not the sound of your voice as the signal to go.

Keep him waiting each time before you tell him to go for the dummy and he will continue to wait for your voice when birds are being used later on.

Lastly, throughout this section we have worked on the assumption that your dog does in fact show interest in wanting to retrieve. The methods I have advised really relate to this type of dog. As to those dogs which do not want to retrieve, I shall discuss these separately in chapter 6 in the section, "Retrieve Problems and Forced Training."

STEADINESS TO SHOT

Steadiness to shot is taught in order to ensure that a dog will not run riot looking for a retrieve each time it hears a gun being discharged—whether that shot has been fired by its owner at a bird it has just pointed or by someone else out of sight. And in the same way that steadiness to a thrown dummy is the first stage of making a dog steady to wing, the exercise we are about to do now is the first stage of teaching a dog to be steady to shot.

Lucky, Maxi, Muppy, and Boone, eager for a morning's training.

This can be taught in two separate stages. The first involves retrieving the dummy when a shot is fired, the dog working from alongside you. The second deals with shots being fired without any retrieving, while the dog is in the course of hunting. So let's take stage one first.

In doing this you are in fact, for the moment, going back to the retrieving exercise and the dog must be standing alongside; as a safeguard, the leash or line is trailing. As before this is simply to ensure, for the first few shots and throws, that the sound of the gun doesn't excite him and tempt him to run in.

It is a good idea now to have a helper fire the pistol and throw the dummy. A member of your own family will be ideal, your wife for instance—provided she isn't gun-shy!

Have your helper stand with the dummy and blank pistol about twenty yards away, to one side and out ahead of you. Command the dog to "whoa." By a prearranged hand signal (rather than a spoken one) the helper will first throw the dummy and then, as it is sailing through the air, fire one pistol shot. Have your foot on the leash in case the dog tries to go for it, though it's very unlikely that he will. Pause for a short time, then send him to pick it up. For this session, repeat this exercise four or five times only. If he hasn't attempted to break, the leash won't be required again.

The next time you go out, allow him two or three retrieves, then have one or two dummies thrown which you or your helper will collect instead. The shot should still be fired each time a dummy is thrown. In addition, you should from time to time fire shots when no dummy is thrown at all. This will puzzle the dog as he will be looking for something to come down, but doing it is important because under normal hunting conditions he will hear shots fired by you or a companion at times when he can't possibly see what has been shot at.

He must not go charging off looking for a retrieve just because he happened to hear a gun fired. Instead, he must stay where he is and await your orders, which subsequently will be either to search for a downed bird ("Fetch") or to ignore matters altogether, before being cast off to hunt again. The command for the latter is the same one you have used when collecting the dummies yourself, i.e., "Gone away," so use it from now on whenever a shot is fired and there is no retrieve. It simply conveys a message which switches his mind off retrieving.

Once you are satisfied that he will stand steady alongside you whenever shots are fired, whether or not retrieves are forthcoming, you may consider moving on to the second stage, which takes place while he is hunting.

Return to the area where you taught him to hunt and quarter. Have only the pistol with you now and cast him off to hunt. You already know he will stop and stand to the "whoa" command while quartering, so you have already done most of the groundwork. All you are doing now is introducing the pistol into the scheme of things. This time, on giving him the usual command to "whoa" while he's hunting out ahead of you, raise your right hand holding the pistol and fire a shot. Because of what you have already done with him close alongside you there should be no problem. But be sure to correct him in the time-honored way if there is—don't let him get away with anything!

Having fired the shot, before you give him the command to hunt on, i.e., "Get on," remember to tell him "Gone away."

When you have had two or three sessions of this using both

the verbal command and the shot, try using the shot only. I think you will be pleasantly surprised by your dog's reaction.

This second stage can also be used with dogs which do not, or will not be required to, retrieve. Up until now you will have done precisely the same with a dog of this type as has been done with one that *will* retrieve, with the exception of course of dummy work. He has been taught to hunt and quarter and to ''whoa'' on command, so all that is necessary now is to incorporate the use of the pistol with his quartering, in precisely the way I have described. At least with a nonretriever the temptation to run in has never been a problem.

Because of all the hard work you have done up to this point, you will be surprised how soon a dog will catch on to it.

Faults

FEAR OF THE GUN

I have found that there is a tendency for people to speak of gun shyness too readily, any sign of fear on the part of a potential gun dog being attributed to this. More often than not, their diagnosis is quite incorrect.

Fear of the gun or, as I term it, "gun nervousness," is in fact more likely the problem and this is quite different from true gun shyness.

Any good potential gun dog, if not introduced to the sound of gunfire in a thoughtful and sensible manner when young, can easily be made gun-nervous. I have in mind such actions as taking a young, inexperienced dog out hunting and firing several shots over it to see how it reacts; doing the same when the young pup bumps into and flushes a cock pheasant, or taking the puppy to a skeet-and-trap range and walking it along behind the guns.

All thoughtless actions of this kind can result in promising young gun dogs' becoming gun-nervous, which in turn leads to other problems, such as blinking, refusal to retrieve, and downright refusal to hunt.

If, however, a dog exhibits early in life a natural and instinctive love of hunting, pointing, and retrieving, the likelihood is that in the right hands gun nervousness can be cured in time by exploiting the natural inbred traits I have mentioned. Even so the outcome will depend to a large extent upon whether or not the problem was quickly identified by the owner and, if so, whether he blithely continued on or immediately stopped everything and sought advice.

Gun nervousness is very definitely, therefore, a man-made fault whereas true gun shyness usually is not. Only rarely does one come across a dog which is gun-shy in the fullest sense of the term.

Gun shyness is apparent when a dog runs away in sheer terror, on hearing a shot, ignoring all commands to return. Sudden noise of any kind can affect it in the same way, not just the sound of a gun. Those very few dogs I have come across that were really gun-shy were inclined to be of a highly sensitive and nervous temperament anyway. Very few dogs indeed are so chronically affected and I believe those that are were born that way.

Those who claim, therefore, to have cured gun-shy dogs in all probability have not done so at all. They have, more likely than not, cured potentially good working dogs that were affected only by gun nervousness.

It is also assumed by many people that, whenever a dog exhibits fear of thunder or firecrackers, this is a sure indication that gun problems are going to be encountered. This isn't so at all. It indicates only that the dog is scared of thunder and firecrackers, and quite possibly nothing else. I can't recall a dog that was particularly fond of either, frankly. Many experienced gun dogs will sit quite happily in a confined blind waiting for ducks and geese to flight while a twelve-gauge shotgun is being discharged only a few feet away, yet be very upset by these other sounds. Firecrackers should never be discharged in the vicinity of a dog of any age. Thunder is unfortunately a phenomenon over which we have no control.

Any young dog will, similarly, exhibit signs of apprehension with any sudden loud noise, especially one close by. So early in life it is both unpleasant and incomprehensible. Take the case of a gun being fired. There is no way that a puppy can possibly understand that something that makes such a terrible din is in fact associated with something he will later enjoy, i.e., hunting. He will come to learn that, of course, but it is essential that the process leading up to this awareness be gradual and that no sense of fear be instilled. If it is done thoughtlessly at first, his instinctive desire for self-preservation will tell him to get away from it if it happens again. Thus great care should be exercised, as outlined in chapter 4.

To start right and as a result have no problems develop is obviously preferable to spending anxious weeks coaxing a puppy around because of something done thoughtlessly.

The section on "Blinking" in this chapter advises how to deal with a case of gun nervousness, as blinking often results from this among other factors.

HARD MOUTH

"Hard mouth" is a serious problem which is generally accepted as being hereditary but which can also to a certain extent be man-made. Defined, the term simply means the crushing of a bird when retrieving it by breaking its rib cage. I have known very few truly incorrigible hard-mouthed dogs, but those that I have come across have had mouths like bear traps, resulting in pulped and mangled carcasses. A dog of this type is quite worthless and not only should be discarded but also should never be bred from.

One should be able to expect from any dog, if he is going to retrieve at all, that he will bring back to hand a dead or wounded bird in no worse condition than when he picked it up.

All manner of weird and wonderful ideas abound which, it is claimed, will cure this problem. But all they would ever prove to me is that such a dog might not, and I stress *might not*, bite down quite so hard while corrective measures were actually being employed. Dogs quickly get wise to all these little tricks in precisely the same way they do with check lines and electric collars and the chances are that the same dog, though persuaded to carry a bird properly while it is being corrected, will very soon revert to his old wicked ways when away from the training field. Quite frankly, no method exists to cure hard mouth permanently.

Hard mouth though should not be confused with the tendency exhibited by some pups to be rough at times when picking up and carrying dummies or birds. Excitement can cause this, particularly in the early days of retrieving birds. And if this does show up, with most it will just as surely disappear as more experience is gained. This is why I advise that retrieving with dummies, preferably of the canvas type, be the very first step with a young dog. An inanimate object like this tends to teach him to hold and carry properly.

Throwing sticks and the like should never be resorted to if you want to avoid mouth problems. Most dogs chew on sticks. Children in particular can't resist playing tug-o-war with the dog. Pulling on one end of a stick while a dog grips and pulls on the other isn't conducive to eventual soft mouth, as I'm sure you will agree.

Common sense is the key to success. Allow retrieving to be done only under supervision in the way I have described. Fool around with it at your peril. You must live with the consequences.

Retrieving cold dead birds (preferably pigeons) comes after dummy retrieving has been perfected. However, with the pointing breeds, unlike flushing dogs, I advise that any retrieving with actual birds be left until after staunchness and steadiness have been accomplished. The temptation to run in and seize the bird before it flies will be that much less.

Beware of the dog which when retrieving bites down so hard that it repeatedly punctures the canvas. This can mean problems ahead. On the other hand, a dog which picks up the dummy hesitantly and occasionally drops it on the way back to you is in all probability a very soft-mouthed animal.

If you have a biter, try to deal with him by placing the dummy in his mouth and walking him on the leash while he carries it. Watch him very carefully and check any attempt by him to roll and mouth the dummy by tapping him under the jaw and saying "No." If you get to the stage where he will carry it alongside you correctly, start moving away from him and calling him to you. Gradually increase the distance, still leaving the leash to trail along (that psychological link) until you feel confident you have corrected the problem.

If he persists, there is no alternative but to give him something else to carry. There may be something he would prefer and you can only find this out by trial and error.

Failing all this there really is no alternative but to try a few dead-bird retrieves to see how he handles them. But remember that this is being done only so that you can definitely determine whether he really is hard-mouthed. If so, I repeat that there's no point in continuing to train him.

I recommend that cold dead birds be used. They are inclined to be stiff and the wings are tight, which helps discourage a dog from playing with the bird and throwing it about. Make sure that they are also free of blood. If this works and you are getting fairly good retrieves, leave it at that. You may well have a dog that doesn't particularly care for dummy-retrieving but is quite willing to bring birds. If this is so, accept things as they are and put the dummy permanently back in the cupboard.

I prefer that no young dog be allowed his first few bird retrieves on pheasants. Apart from the fact that pheasants are large and can be difficult for an inexperienced dog to pick up, a wounded cock bird can easily spur a dog in the muzzle, and anyone who has experienced a jab in the wrist from this source will appreciate the sensation. Being beaten about the head by a pair of wings also isn't the best thing in the world for a youngster. Either experience can result in one of two things happening: (1) refusal for a long time to pick up another bird, or (2) holding the bird down on the ground and killing it. And how would he kill it? He would do so by crushing the ribs across the back, hence the start of hard mouth, as he will in all probability from then on consider this to be the perfect solution each time a cripple has to be retrieved. Once this has started, you will never be able to stop it.

There will be times when a dog will return to you with a pheasant (a live one, perhaps) which is found to have either teeth punctures in the breast or torn skin at the base of the tail. This is not an indication that your dog is hard-mouthed. Damage of this sort can occur as the result of a bird's being wounded when it has fallen into dense, thorny cover from which the dog has had considerable difficulty extracting it. He has perhaps had to drag it while backing out of the cover and therefore had to hold onto the bird harder than would otherwise be necessary. So don't think the worst if this happens.

Unless a dog is truly hard-mouthed by heredity, as few are, retrieving exercises conducted correctly from the start will usually prevent problems of rough bird-handling or hard mouth.

Finally, if after all you believe that your dog may indeed be hard-mouthed and you want to be quite sure about this before deciding whether to carry on training him, contact a professional trainer and ask him if he will take the dog for a couple of weeks for an opinion. Whatever the outcome, it will be worth doing as you will then be sure.

RETRIEVE PROBLEMS AND FORCED TRAINING

We have already covered certain problems relating to retrieving in discussing hard mouth. Separating these two matters is somewhat difficult but I have endeavored to refer in the section on ''Hard Mouth'' only to those aspects of retrieving which can lead to this problem or, if you are lucky, prevent it.

There are other problems connected with retrieving, however, which are not linked to hard mouth. They relate to a lack of desire to retrieve.

I have stated before that, where the pointing breeds are concerned, retrieving can be a very unpredictable talent and that, if any pointing dog retrieves well, not only should it be taken as an added bonus but the dog is worth its weight in gold.

Jason, a German shorthaired pointer who is owned by a good friend of mine, is one of this type. He retrieves to hand as well as any labrador and never damages a feather on any bird he collects, dead or alive. Retrieving of that quality by any dog of any breed is always a pleasure to see.

However, the fact must be faced that some pointing dogs lack the interest to retrieve altogether. I will get back to the nonretrievers shortly and will concentrate for the moment on those that are just inclined to be sloppy or indifferent.

If you do detect in your dog a tendency to lack interest in

retrieving the dummy, try something else. Use a glove or a slipper and, if it increases his interest, stick with it. Never be tempted to overdo this, especially with a dog that has to be persuaded. If you can get one or two nice pickups and deliveries to hand each time, no matter what you use, then leave it at that. The fact that he is at least going out and picking up and delivering *something* to you is achieving the object of the exercise, namely, delivery to hand.

Change of location can sometimes help too. A dog may not react as you would want him to in a certain area, perhaps because he associates that area with something else he wasn't too keen on. Some owners have succeeded by starting a pup in the home and then, once he's carrying satisfactorily, continuing outside.

I have known dogs which show little or no desire to pick up a dummy which is clearly visible, but will hunt eagerly for it when it is thrown into cover out of sight. The latter necessitates nose work to locate it, whereupon it is picked up and carried back willingly.

Bird wings fastened to the dummy with strong rubber bands can often help as they create a sense of the real thing. Any potential gun dog worth his salt should show more interest in feathers, whether on or off the bird! Don't hesitate to try this if all else fails, despite the fact that (at risk of repeating myself) I prefer to leave the "birdy" aspect of things with pointing dogs until later, where actual retrieving is concerned. If I were having the same problem with a retriever or a springer spaniel I would use bird wings without hesitation, and probably dead and live birds too—for example, pigeons with their wing feathers clipped. But training a flushing dog is different from training a pointing dog. The longer the latter is restrained before he gets his mouth around a bird, the more effective steadiness training will be.

Sometimes a dog will pick up a dummy, then stand and refuse to bring it to you. Edible rewards can occasionally help with this problem, but only if absolutely necessary as they can result in the dog's mind being tuned to only one thing, the goody itself. This in turn often leads to the annoying habit of the dog's dropping the dummy part way back in anticipation of the food. However, if only the food trick will work, use it.

Where refusal to return with the dummy is concerned, you

should also consider the use of the check line. Clip the line on, then throw the dummy within the range of the line itself. On sending the dog, hold onto the other end of the line. As he picks up the dummy, give a sharp tug and call him. Don't pull or drag him or he will drop the dummy immediately. As he comes trotting towards you, move back and still hold onto the end of the line while drawing it in as he gets nearer. You are then in a position to give another tug if he stops and looks as though he's going to act up again. All the time he's coming in keep quiet, and praise him only when he actually gets to you, not before. The line will continue to be necessary for two or three weeks.

What you must look for to indicate that things are beginning to work is the moment when, without that tug on the line, he picks up and starts coming towards you on his own initiative. At that time, but not before, you can consider replacing the line with the short leather leash and eventually removing the choke chain too.

If you have a dog with a sensitive disposition, your problem may well be due to the fact that you are unconsciously dominating him by eye contact. This can indeed happen. Try therefore to avoid staring directly in his eyes as he is coming towards you. This can be very intimidating with certain dogs, causing them to slow down or make a detour around you. Just lower your eyes as you back away and talk him in using a quiet, encouraging tone.

If your dog does not learn to retrieve well yet seems fine in all other respects, you may wish to consider "forced retrieve training." This is a specialized technique which, if done incorrectly by someone who does not understand its application, can bring about lasting harm. Therefore I have no intention of explaining here how it is taught. I would simply advise you to talk to a professional trainer. If done correctly it can work very well indeed, but not all professionals deal with this. However, any trainer will at least be able to tell you of someone who does.

BLINKING

Of all the problems that are likely to arise during the training of gun dogs of any breed, "blinking" is perhaps the most difficult to detect in its early stages, as it usually develops slowly and unobtrusively over a period of time. The term simply relates to the tendency in a dog to ignore the presence of game while hunting despite the fact that he has scented it and is aware it is there.

Dogs which develop this fault manifest it in various ways. One may, while hunting with drive and enthusiasm, stop and point for just a few seconds, then slowly back off and turn away; whereupon he resumes hunting with the same zest as before. Another may, on detecting the bird, point normally but then, before the handler has had time to walk up close, back off as the first dog did. However, this one instead of resuming hunting will, with tail and head down, slowly walk back towards his handler as though unsure or afraid of the consequences of having found the bird. A third dog, perhaps the most difficult to come to grips with, will merely acknowledge the presence of a bird by a sudden, almost undetectable movement of the head as he sweeps by and gets scent. There will in all probability be no stopping, not even for a flash point, but instead just a slight acknowledgment as he continues on his way.

The cause of this reaction will almost certainly be something which occurred in the course of training. In other words, I believe blinking is a man-made fault and that it usually arises as a direct result of one of two training indiscretions, that is, careless introduction to the gun, thereby causing gun nervousness, or pushing a young dog to do too much too soon while employing methods which for that particular dog's disposition are too tough and overbearing.

In the case of careless introduction to the gun, it is quite likely that blinking birds will not become a problem until one actually starts to shoot over the dog, which in correct training sequence will be after the dog is staunch on point. Only when the gun is fired to shoot a bird which it has pointed will this association form in the dog's mind: If he finds a bird and holds the point, his handler will flush the bird, which will result in that terrible noise he has disliked so much since he first heard it as a puppy. Otherwise stated, he has associated the *bang* with the *bird* and reasons that, if he *doesn't* indicate the bird's presence, his handler will not flush it and consequently the bird won't "explode." Far better, therefore, to ignore its presence and hunt on!

When careless introduction of the gun is, accordingly, the problem, the only line of action one can take is to go right back to square one with the gun and follow the advice I outlined earlier. It will be time-consuming and there's no guarantee of success, of course, so how much better it would have been had everything been done right in the first place!

The other example I gave, too early and too tough a training approach, can also be fairly attributed to thoughtlessness. The problem invariably arises during steadiness training, usually because one has failed to understand what type of dog one is dealing with. By this I mean whether he is bold and an extrovert or a shy, quiet character lacking in confidence. Each requires an entirely different approach, as I have explained before, but even the dog possessing a bold dispositon will suffer adversely if too hard a hand is used in training.

Again we are back to temper and therefore voice control, and in this regard it is most important, especially where actual work over birds is concerned, that a threatening tone of voice never be used. When a dog is pointing, the "whoa" command should be given in a quiet, soothing manner and rough handling to staunch a dog should be avoided at all costs.

The remedy this time can in fact be far more difficult to effect than with the other cause, since in this case it means that you must cultivate a totally different attitude and approach towards your dog. Not only do you have to go back and start all over again but you must, in doing so, be prepared to adopt a gentler training manner, involving the exercise of more patience than so far has been displayed.

You may even have to ask yourself whether you lack the temperament to train a dog successfully. Only you will know the answer to this. But if you do, then let a professional do the job for you. Your dog will enjoy itself far more and will then be likely to reach his potential.

FLAGGING ON POINT

Little can be said about the habit some dogs have of "flagging''—waving or wagging their tail while on point. In some instances, it should never have started in the first place. And in most cases, nothing can be done to effectively cure it.

This fault is hereditary in some dogs and with those you can bet your life it is going to stay that way. With others, flagging is man-made. Some dogs flag from the moment they go on point while others only do so as the handler walks in close to flush the bird. In either case it is quite likely that flagging has been caused by the owner himself.

Some people have the habit of continually talking to their dogs. They simply cannot shut up. Because of this, some dogs which otherwise might never have started to flag will begin to do so. For instance, the dog may be subjected to a nonstop barrage of: "Whoa boy," "That's a good feller," "Steady now, whoa," "Easy now," "That's the idea," and so on!

Flagging will develop far more quickly in a dog that is overaffectionate by nature. Talking to him in this way will be interpreted as praise, which naturally results in tail-wagging. Once a dog is on point, the handler should keep his mouth shut other than to give a quiet, firm "Whoa" when necessary. Nothing else. If the dog is pointing staunchly, then why on earth keep nagging him to do what he's already doing? It is absolutely unnecessary and usually spoils what is already being done very well.

Flagging by any dog in trials is especially abhorred. Otherwise, I will concede that flagging by a gun dog doesn't matter so much, especially if he's a good all-rounder otherwise. After all, he's not required to point with his tail!

7

Use of Birds
in Training

QUAIL AND CHUKAR PARTRIDGE

Bobwhite quail are perhaps the most traditional bird for pointing-dog trainers as a relatively small number can be housed and used over and over again in training. They are also "gamey" and hold well for a dog.

I have already (in chapter 3) described the quail call-back pen and how it operates. For the man who has only one or two pointing dogs to train or keep up to standard, about a dozen quail can easily be kept in a small, portable pen.

I suggest purchasing birds that are over eight weeks old if possible. They are available at most game farms and when first obtained should be confined to the call-back pen for a week or ten days to become thoroughly familiar with their surroundings. This will increase your chances of their returning to the pen by late in the day after they have been released.

The pen should be sited if possible in a shady area out on the training ground. At first, in order to train the birds, only two or three of them should be released at a time. They are best not worked by the dog for the time being. When they return to the pen late in the day, encouraged by the calling of the cock birds left behind, they can be kept for the moment in the bottom section of the pen, to which they gained access via the reentry tunnel. Another two or three can be released from the top section the following day, and so on. After they have all been out and have returned, training with them may start.

Depending upon the type and size of the pen and the amount of land you have on which to train, it may be necessary for you to carry the pen back to your home each evening, after the birds released earlier have returned. If, however, you have a larger, vermin-proof pen and sufficient ground to allow you to leave it in situ all the time, you have no problem.

You should start by releasing six to eight birds the first thing in the morning on the day you are going to do some training. Be sure to leave at least one or two cocks in the pen as they will be responsible for calling the others back. Without these callback birds, the chances of getting the others to return are extremely remote.

As they fly away from the pen, try to mark each well wherever it lands, then leave them for an hour or so before getting the dog out to hunt them. The purpose of leaving them alone for a while is to allow them time to move around and spread some scent in the cover.

As each bird is flushed after the dog has pointed, try not to follow up the same bird more than twice, as pen-reared quail, especially young birds, soon weaken if flushed too many times. This increases the possibility of the dog's breaking point and trapping the bird before it has a chance to fly. This should be avoided at all costs.

It helps if you purchase your birds from a breeder who rears them in good, long flight pens. Some game farm operators will purposely go to the pen several times daily and shake the wire, thereby causing the birds to flush and fly the length of the pen, maybe fifty yards or more. This strengthens their wings and good flyers are the result. Those reared in cramped conditions could be poor birds on which to train. Any bird getting up and flying only a very short distance and landing again in sight of the dog can be a source of trouble when training. When the birds fly well for a good distance before alighting, there is less temptation for the dog to break and chase.

Four or five points can be completed in a morning on birds released this way, and maybe another three or four during the early afternoon. I think it best to leave them alone after that so that they can regain their composure before making their way home. If chivvied about and flown too often, or too late in the day, they will probably roost out all night and possibly fall prey to a passing fox or hunting owl.

I think it's a good idea to leave the pen in the same area if possible, provided you find things work well from there. If problems do arise, only trial and error will reveal the best spot. This way the birds will get to know their territory better, which is an important factor in self-preservation. Any game bird in territory it knows well will have a greater chance of survival when predators are around, as they will be capable of flying to safety when the need arises.

Coturnix quail are also often used but they are not as good as bobwhite quail. They are slightly smaller, usually fly less well, and will not return as well as bobwhite to a call-back pen.

Chukar partridge, however, can be used to very good effect in much the same way as bobwhite quail. They are usually good flyers and respond to a call-back very well as a rule. Like quail, they tend to hold well for a dog.

Apart from their value for training, quail are nice birds to have around anyway. Being out in the fields on a quiet summer evening listening to the cocks calling to one another is always a delightful experience.

PIGEONS

I talked about quail first and referred to them as the traditional training bird for pointing breeds, as indeed I think they are. But having expressed that opinion, I will also say that in many respects I consider pigeons to be just as good.

Like quail, pigeons are fairly easily obtainable. You can usually get culled birds from racing enthusiasts or from livestock auctions. In addition they can be trapped inside barns and silos;

farmers usually will gladly give permission for them to be caught if only because of the awful mess they make.

Ten or fifteen pigeons can be easily housed and if they are of the right type, i.e., homers, once accustomed to their new environment they will invariably fly right back to their loft after being released. Bear in mind, however, that if released too soon they'll head right back to their *original* home, thus necessitating another trip to buy more birds.

All you require is a fly-back box of the type shown in the sketch, in which can be placed food and water. It should have on the outside a platform on which the birds can land, and set into the side of the box there should be a light-alloy swinging gate through which the birds can push their way back in. It is essential that the gate be of the lightest metal and that it only swing inwards.

I tend to prefer pigeons for starting a young dog (flushing dog as well as pointer) because they get up and fly so well when flushed and, once airborne, keep going right back to the coop.

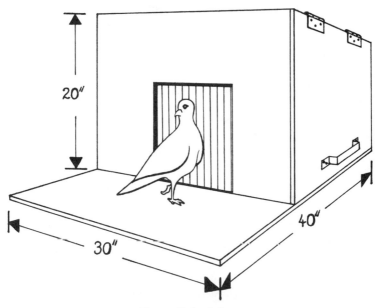

Pigeon fly-back box.

The dog's concentration is then broken and he can forget each bird and revert to hunting again.

Their scent, albeit not gamey, nevertheless brings out the point in most dogs, although I will admit that with the occasional dog its point can be softer and less stylish with pigeons. But this reservation rarely applies until they have been worked for some time on game; usually only then will a dog show less interest in pigeon scent. The vast majority of dogs, after working game, will still react with enthusiasm once back in a training session with pigeons.

If it is always borne in mind that the use of pigeons is strictly for training, and that once this has been accomplished experience on the real thing must be sought, pigeons are well worth using. Indeed, I have always maintained that if a gun dog of any breed will retrieve pigeons consistently well, he will retrieve any other bird that is shot for him.

I do not subscribe to the theory, incidentally, that some dogs don't like the smell or taste of woodcock and because of this will not retrieve them. I believe that any dog that refuses to retrieve woodcock isn't a reliable retriever anyway, and will probably refuse from time to time to pick up other types of game as well. The taste-and-scent theory is, I think, an excuse for a poor all-around retriever. Any dog that really loves to retrieve will pick up and carry anything that is shot over him, including rabbits and hares, as many gun dogs in Britain are required to do, pointing breeds included.

In short, a few pigeons housed as I have suggested, in a fly-back box attached to the side of a barn or shed, will give excellent service and can be used over and over. Incidentally, be sure to give them a good supply of grit along with their food. Presently in this chapter we will go into the way in which they should be used.

PHEASANTS

I like pheasants. I think a ring-necked cock pheasant in prime condition in the fall is the most beautiful of all game birds and a most exciting one to hunt. However, they should be hunted only after a dog has gained experience in pointing and retrieving all the birds I have mentioned. My reasons for saying this have been clearly spelled out in chapter 6 in the section on "Hard Mouth."

This advice I give for all breeds including that best-suited of all gun dogs for this very sporting bird, the English springer spaniel.

To try to confuse the dogs, pheasants tend to run away rather than fly; consequently, unless confined to a release cage during training, this is precisely what they will do under pressure if the cover conditions are suitable. They will move yard by yard through the undergrowth, forcing a dog to frequently break point and relocate, which for an inexperienced dog is hardly conducive to gaining staunchness. This not only results in the loss of more birds than you finish up getting points on, but it is also going to lead to frustration on your part and the habit, quickly learned by any dog, of ground-scent trailing. This you must try to avoid. A pointing dog's head should be held high when hunting and quartering, not glued to the ground trying to locate and follow foot scent.

Thus, of all the different types of bird on which a bird dog can be trained, I strongly recommend leaving pheasants until last. If you do, you will have better results when you get around to working your dog on pheasants later.

BIRD PLANTING AND RELEASE CAGES

I venture to suggest that one may justifiably describe bird planting for the purpose of gun-dog training as a minor art! It is a technique that has come about over the years for the following reasons.

It is a fact of life that no matter where gun-dog training is undertaken, much of that training, especially that relating to bird work, has to be of an artificial nature. And it is perhaps better that it be that way where the instilling of discipline and control is concerned.

Lucky indeed is the man who is able to walk out from his home and work his dog on plenty of wild birds in good cover conditions. Only those with access to a shooting preserve tend to come close to this ideal, but even those birds are not wild in the true

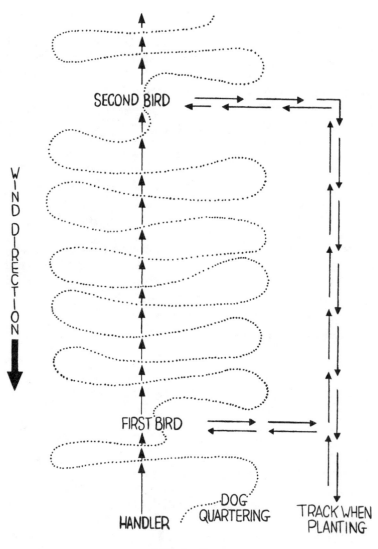

WIND DIRECTION

SECOND BIRD

FIRST BIRD

HANDLER

DOG QUARTERING

TRACK WHEN PLANTING

Bird planting.

sense of the term. They are in fact pen-released birds that for the most part may have been roaming free only for the previous few days.

Professional trainers are affected in precisely the same way as their busiest time of the year is, more often than not, between hunting seasons.

Bird planting for training has therefore become a necessity.

I have already described the different types of bird that can be used for training bird dogs and in doing so I have outlined the use of the call-back-pen system for quail or chukar and the fly-back box for homing pigeons. So now we will go into the use of these birds in the field, employing methods other than that of releasing quail from a call-back pen. If quail are being used but a call-back pen is not feasible, then it will be necessary either to take them out in a crate and drop them one at a time into suitable cover, in the way I have described in chapter 4, "First Points," or to use a release cage.

Release cages can be purchased from most training equipment suppliers. Some incorporate a movable center section which allows two birds to be put in at one time. However, this is for multiple bird releases, which aren't either necessary or advisable until staunchness and steadiness have been instilled. The cage has a spring-loaded lid which flies open when a metal arm is depressed. It can also be triggered from a distance, while a dog is pointing, by a length of cord attached to the release arm.

After the quail is placed in the cage it should be taken out to the training field. In fact, at least two cages should be used preferably and they should be concealed in the grass at least seventy-five yards apart. The fact that the bird can move about freely inside the cage helps to create more scent. The dog is then brought out and hunted and, on his locating and pointing the bird, the lever is activated either by foot or by the cord, the lid springs open, and the bird flies off. This method ensures that all birds used are found and pointed and that, if a dog is inclined to be unsteady on point, he can't dive in and catch the bird.

More sophisticated cages are available should your dog be of the type I have just mentioned. These have a folding canvas sling in which the bird is placed prior to the lid being secured. The difference with this cage though is that, on being activated, the strength of the spring mechanism is such that the canvas sling is pulled tight and the bird is literally catapulted several feet into the air, at which point it flies off. The speed at which the bird is thrown up into the air reduces even further the chances of a dog's catching it before it gets airborne.

There is also the electronically operated type that is triggered from a distance by a transmitter. This type is very effective without doubt, but of course expensive and hardly necessary for the one- or two-dog man.

The latter two are most useful in helping to correct the fault of a dog's breaking point and trying to catch the bird. It's not too long before a persistent breaker begins to realize he's wasting his time.

The same type of cage can be used for planting pigeons also. A double quail cage holds, as an alternative, one pigeon and all that one has to do is unclip and lower the dividing section in the middle.

With certain types of pigeon there is a tendency, once the top springs open, for the bird to stay there and not fly immediately. Usually the smaller, fancier type of bird will do this whereas the big blue homers or barn-trapped wild birds will be out and away without a moment's hesitation.

As an alternative to using the cages, one can plant pigeons by hand. This means first dizzying the bird slightly, then tucking its head beneath a wing, after which it should be laid down gently in a suitable patch of cover. When touched later, it will rouse itself, stand up, and be ready for flight. If planted correctly, it will stay precisely where you placed it until you hunt the dog—as long as fifteen or twenty minutes or more.

I like this system and in general prefer it to using cages, but I will of course use cages whenever I think it might be better for a particular dog; for instance, one that isn't yet as staunch as it should be.

When a pigeon is planted in this way, probably less scent surrounds it than would be the case if it were moving around inside a cage. But to compensate for that the flush is more natural.

Some people express concern about hand scent on a bird which has been planted and will use gloves, thinking to avoid it. In my opinion, this is quite ineffective as the glove itself is

Dizzying a pigeon . . .

. . . the head is then tucked beneath the wing . . .

. . . and the bird is gently placed in suitable cover.

Alternatively, the pigeon may be placed in a release cage . . .

... after which the spring-loaded lid is secured and the cage concealed.

Quail being released from a call-back pen prior to a training session.

saturated with human scent. This will in turn be transferred to the bird, thereby defeating the object of the exercise.

You should always remember when planting pigeons not to place them in cover too deep or too thick. The reason for this is as follows: Pigeons use only their wings to take flight, unlike game birds (particularly pheasants), which use the strength of their legs to good effect to spring up. A pigeon in cover is therefore at some disadvantage and will be easily caught by a dog before it has the chance to get airborne. So allow them space to get away.

Let me add another important point to be borne in mind when bird planting, whether by hand or in cages. You should make every effort to avoid creating a trail of your own foot scent right up the center of the field. For instance, we will assume that you are going out to place either two pigeons or two quail to be hunted up by the dog. You are hand-planting them, therefore carrying them in a bag or small crate.

The object is to plant them so that the minimum amount of foot scent is left, as dogs quickly learn that your track leads to birds and once this has dawned on them they'll start to trail you if they can get away with it. This can be avoided by walking up the outside edge of the field or area to be hunted, then into the field to the point at which you plant the first bird. Return to the outside edge along the same route and continue further, walking in once more to plant the second. The birds can be set at, say, fifty to seventy-five yards apart. You should then return down the edge of the field to your starting point.

By doing this, you will keep foot scent to a minimum and thus ensure that your dog will hunt and quarter without resorting to trailing. See the sketch on this for a clearer picture of what I have just explained.

In conclusion, I must emphasize that, although fine for training dogs, no artificially planted bird will ever be a truly satisfactory substitute for eventual experience on wild birds. However, circumstances dictate that pen-raised birds be used if gun dogs are to be trained at all. Used properly, they contribute a great deal towards this end and help produce a gun dog that, when hunted on wild birds later, will do so under good control.

8

Advanced Training

POINTING AND STAUNCHNESS

You are now at that stage where some serious bird work can commence, the object being to teach your dog to become staunch on point.

There is often a tendency for people to confuse *staunchness* with *steadiness*, but the two are quite different. A dog that is *staunch* is one that will stand and hold his point on a bird allowing you time to approach and flush it. A dog that is *steady* is one that will remain standing still until ordered to retrieve once a bird has been flushed and shot.

Many hunters, of course, are not really interested in whether their dog is steady to wing and shot, being quite satisfied if it will hold the point staunchly until the bird is flushed. Others ask that their dog hold until the shot is fired, whereupon the dog runs in for the retrieve without command. And as I've commented before, whatever is done is fine just as long as it satisfies the owner.

However, at this stage we are concerned only with staunchness. The attaining of steadiness will follow.

If quail are being used from a call-back pen already set out on your training area, go out first and release five or six birds and note approximately where each lands. Always make sure when a call-back pen is being used that you keep your dog or dogs away from the pen itself. Do not train in its immediate vicinity. If you do the dog will quickly "wise up" to its significance and will want to head for it at every opportunity.

If on the other hand you will be using quail in release cages, then it will be necessary to walk out beforehand and place two or three cages, each containing a bird, out in the field in the way I have already described.

Precisely the same applies if pigeons are being used and, for the purpose of this exercise, let's presume that they are and that you are going to place the first in a release cage and plant the second, with its head under its wing, in light cover. Having set the birds out, return to the kennel or the car and get the dog. Never allow a dog to watch what you are doing.

Now, although you may well have your dog under good control by this time, I strongly sugggest that the check line still be used as a safeguard, because it is vitally important that the dog not get the opportunity to break and catch the bird before it flies. Despite the fact that he has been taught the "whoa" command thoroughly, so far he has only been tempted to break by thrown dummies. Now we are advancing a stage further. Birds are being used, so the temptation is far greater. So as not to push your luck too far, slip the choke chain and check line on.

Start the dog hunting well downwind of the first bird to allow him time, when cast off, to quarter his way up the field before he gets to his first point. Keep him close in and be ready, as he passes across and downwind of the bird, to give the "whoa" command if necessary as he stops and begins to point. But only use the command if, after stopping, he starts to move in closer to the bird. He should be prevented at all costs from creeping forward. If he still fails to hold properly, step on the line to jerk him to a standstill and, at the same moment, give the command "Whoa" a second time. No need to yell it, just give it in a firm, clear tone of voice. Then pick him up bodily and move him back to where he was when he first detected scent. Set him up there

Having removed the check line, it is advisable to leave the choke chain on until reliable staunchness has been achieved.

Too close to the release cage, which also should have been concealed better!

and repeat the command.

There will be times under certain conditions relating to scent strength, wind direction, and so on when a dog will get only a very slight whiff of scent, then nothing more. This will call for relocating in order to get a more positive find. It may only mean a move of a yard or less, but this is a matter you will come to recognize with experience as being a move quite different from just creeping in to get closer. This is called "reading" your dog. The better you get to know dogs, the more proficient you will become at this.

However, we will presume that he has stopped and held point of his own accord with just one reminder from you. As he is holding the point, you always approach him from the side or front and not from directly behind. A dog approached from behind may get a little uneasy and move around, whereas the same dog, if you come up on him from an angle that enables him to see you, will continue to hold his point staunchly.

With the majority of dogs, one may move in close alongside and stroke the dog's back against the lie of the hair, or push the dog gently into the point, so that he reacts by locking up tighter. However, there are others which, when this is done, soften up immediately, relax their point, and even start to flag their tails. If this reaction becomes apparent, discontinue touching him altogether; to persist will make matters worse. Some dogs don't like or don't need such encouragement, while others do. So it's up to you to watch carefully and assess your particular dog's needs.

Now is a good time to recruit a helper again. This is because for the present it is essential that you stand alongside your dog, concentrating on him with one foot pressed firmly down on the line so that, should he break when the bird is flushed, you are still in control. Obviously, if you are doing this, you cannot at the same time walk forward to flush the bird. To do so would risk the dog's making a lunge when you were unable to prevent it.

Let's take a look at both eventualities, then, and discuss what should be done depending upon whether the dog breaks or holds his point.

When you are positioned and ready, indicate to your helper by nodding (avoid speaking if possible) to walk in and flush the bird. Of course, he does so from the front or side of the dog. At the moment the cage is sprung or the bird is pushed out of the cover, give the "Whoa" command and brace yourself in case he does decide to break, and in this instance we will assume that he does. Now at this juncture I must point out that we are in fact getting involved with "steadiness to wing," the subject of the next section of this chapter. The present reference is unavoidable though as it bears directly on the action necessary to counteract the break.

From the moment the dog starts to run in, discipline yourself to say nothing. Don't be tempted to yell at him. Just let the line zip out until he suddenly discovers there's no more left and he is dumped head over tail. Haul him back immediately to where he was and set him up again despite the fact that the bird has gone. Now tell him "Whoa" once more. Make sure he stands there twenty seconds or so, then, remembering to say "Gone away," heel him off away from the direction in which the bird departed and cast him off to hunt towards the second bird.

What I have described here illustrates again the importance of the check line at each stage until you are satisfied it is no longer required. It is needed only for a short time. In this instance, without the line you might have had a situation in which (a) he caught the bird as it took off, or (b) he engaged in a long and futile chase. And you definitely want to avoid both.

In addition, I have emphasized the desirability of not speaking or yelling at your dog once he has broken and until you have him back in control again. This is so that, when he is bowled over by the check line, he will regard the bird as being responsible, not you. This train of thought will quickly result in his remaining staunch.

If on the other hand he remains steady when the bird flushes, as a result of the control you have instilled in him, let him stand there until the bird is out of sight. Praise him, say "Gone away," heel him off as recommended before, then cast him off to work the second bird.

The purpose of heeling the dog away and saying "Gone away" is of course to get his mind off the departing bird. If you were to cast him off immediately from where he stood it might well cause a chase, as he could presume that you had told him he could. Walking away a few yards first in a different direction will help considerably to reduce that possibility.

It is now that the usefulness of the "Gone away" command will be fully appreciated!

Every effort must be made at this time to prevent the dog from getting in too close and "eyeballing" the bird; in other words, looking where it is. He must be taught to use his nose and not his eyes, and to react accordingly by pointing as a result of locating scent alone. A dog permitted to keep looking for birds will never staunch up well and will always tend to get in too close and crowd the birds, thereby risking wild flushes.

Sometimes a close point can't be avoided when the dog happens to swing close by and downwind of the bird. Irrespective of the distance, however, the dog should slam on the brakes and point anyway—even if the bird is only six inches from the end of his nose! In this instance, provided he locks up and holds, nothing was done incorrectly at all; in fact, his reaction is to be praised. By stopping so promptly and holding so well he has exercised skill and caution in the best possible manner. The dog that has to be corrected is the one that wants to use his eyes and get in close, and that's a different thing altogether.

It is particularly important during the process of staunching a dog that your assistant, and in time you yourself, kick around in the cover for a while in the vicinity of the bird before it is pushed out and while the dog is still on point. This is because, when wild birds are being hunted later on, you may not know precisely where they are despite the fact that the dog is on point. This means (unless it's a grouse and very spooky) walking round in front of the dog and kicking the cover for a while before the bird takes off. Take the opportunity, therefore, to do this during training so that your dog gets used to it.

It's no good just walking in and giving a quick flip of the foot so that the bird flies straight away. There must be more temptation than that and, as likely as not, you will notice your dog tense up in anticipation, so be extra vigilant. Every stage in training has its pitfalls, so always try to be one step ahead of your dog.

After a few sessions you will probably find that you can walk around and flush the bird without your dog showing any sign of wanting to break. Do this as soon as you can and continue it just as long as you have confidence he will stand his ground.

In conclusion, a few more tips: Remember the check line-choke chain sequence; remove each again when you feel it's time. Never walk between a dog on point and the bird if you can possibly help it—keep on the outside of the bird if you can, as in this way you are less likely to break the dog's concentration. And don't ever rush up to a dog that's pointing; some people literally run in while uttering a string of meaningless commands in an attempt to exhort the dog to hold. Such tactics will, as likely as not, result in just the opposite response. Excitement on the part of the owner is quickly transmitted to a dog, and this can in turn lead to unsteadiness.

The role of a pointer is to hunt, locate and point birds staunchly, and allow the owner to make a leisurely approach. A pointing dog that will not do this hasn't been trained properly.

STEADINESS TO WING

Teaching steadiness is, by reason of its somewhat exacting requirements, a gradual process which should thread its way through the whole of a dog's training as described in these pages. If a dog is ever to become reliably steady, there are no shortcuts to teaching it.

Most people regard steadiness as the most difficult of all phases of training, and so it would be if you were trying to steady a dog which had received no basic yard training beforehand. However, you are more than halfway towards this goal already. All that remains is to convert the steadiness you taught artificially to steadiness in respect to the real thing—birds. By virtue of the methodical way you have built up to this, you should experience very few problems.

Successful steadiness training depends not only on the trainer's being patient and conscientious, but also on what type of dog the trainer has to work with. If, for instance, you are attempting to steady a dog that is twelve months old or older, which up until this time has received no yard training whatsoever yet has been allowed to hunt and chase birds, then I suggest that any effort you put into it now is going to be futile.

On the other hand, if you are dealing with a young dog which you have reared and brought along as I have suggested in this book, your chances of success are that much better. So let's summarize what you have done so far: Your dog will walk to heel on and off the leash. He will stand and "whoa" when commanded either when alongside you or when running in towards you. And he will do this when quartering in the field. He will stop and "whoa" to hand signal and whistle while quartering and remain steady when you throw dummies and fire shots, waiting until you give the order to retrieve. Lastly, he will point birds staunchly.

You have therefore done a great deal of the groundwork relating to steadiness, which, although so far of an artificial nature, will aid immeasurably when translated into bird work with the gun.

In starting steadiness-to-wing training, therefore, you should begin in precisely the same way as you did when teaching staunchness, that is, by first planting birds out in the field. Once again a helper is advisable, one who has with him a blank pistol for the first session or two, to be followed later by a shotgun.

Hunt your dog up to the first bird, once again with the check line on. When the dog has located and is holding the point, stand on the line, give him a reminder to "whoa," then nod to your helper to release the bird, this time having him fire a shot as it flies off. Be ready to bowl the dog over if he breaks, and put him back where he was in the usual manner. The gun is being used now in conjunction with birds actually flying away from right in front of him, and this will create far more excitement than any canvas dummy ever did.

However, it is precisely because you used the gun in the manner you did in the early days, and because you got him accustomed to hearing it fired while dummies were being thrown, that your firing it now as the bird flies off probably will cause no problems at all. In a sense he's already "steady to shot" and all you are doing is integrating this with "steadiness to wing." Think about it!

When the bird is out of sight, give the "Gone away" command and walk off the usual short distance before casting him off once more for the second, and then if successful the third, bird—each time going through the same methodical procedure.

This must be repeated over and over during several more sessions while your helper does the flushing and shooting. You may then use the shotgun instead of the blank pistol. Your dog has heard it before so he's used to it. But don't be tempted to shoot any birds just yet, as he isn't quite ready for that. For the moment, they must all be allowed to fly off with only a shot fired in the air. We will progress to shooting birds in the next section on "Retrieving."

As with each previous exercise, when all is going well, discard first the check line, then the choke chain, and finally flush the birds and fire the gun yourself. You've discarded the line so this means you're confident your dog will hold satisfactorily. But still keep a wary eye on him! As you're not actually shooting the birds, there's no need at all to watch where the birds go. It is far more important that you watch *your dog* carefully so that you can react quickly as the need arises.

Should a break occur, go out immediately and haul him back to where he was. Once there, he must be shaken up and put on the "whoa" again for a short time before being allowed to move on. Persistent disobedience will simply indicate that you have advanced too rapidly, so be prepared to face up to this and go back a stage or two. It's the only way you'll ever succeed.

This phase should not take long for the reasons I have outlined. As soon as you are satisfied that your dog will remain steady, free of the line, while you flush the bird and fire the shot, without his showing signs of wanting to break, then you can consider moving on to the second stage of steadiness training. This involves actually shooting some birds over the dog and allowing him to retrieve some too.

Now is the time you really will discover whether all you have done so far has been as thorough as it should have been.

RETRIEVING BIRDS

The object in delaying actual bird retrieving was to avoid creating in the dog a desire to pick up and carry birds before he learned to point staunchly and to be steady to wing and shot. To have done this in the opposite order would have resulted in such problems as the dog's looking for the bird instead of using his nose, getting in too close, and worst of all, breaking point in an attempt to catch it.

It is logical, on the other hand, that if the dog is taught in the sequence we have followed here, temptations and therefore problems are less likely to arise. The fact that dummies were used earlier in retrieving is immaterial as the dog will not have connected these with birds. They have merely served to teach him to pick up, carry, and deliver correctly.

As with staunchness and steadiness-to-wing training, it is advisable to use the check line at first and let your helper do the shooting, this time using only the shotgun, as some birds are going to be shot. If you were doing the shooting, your attention would be distracted at the very moment your dog would be most likely to break and run in, which is the time you would have the gun to your shoulder. There is no way you can watch the dog for those few seconds, and he will sense it.

Furthermore, it is most important from this stage in training that both you and your helper be fully aware of two other fundamental principles which must be rigorously observed. These are as follows:

(1) Never shoot a bird over a dog which breaks and runs in as the bird flies. The gunner should always pause first to see that the dog has held before taking the shot. This is because, as I have said before, a retrieve is a reward for doing right. If he breaks, he has done wrong, so no reward should be forthcoming.

(2) Never shoot over a pointing dog a bird which he has not pointed. The bird may, for instance, fly off as the dog is approaching it. If this happens it must be left strictly alone with no shot fired. When hunting wild birds later, there are bound to be occasions when a bird will flush which the dog has not pointed. This will happen often with grouse and sometimes with pheasent. Woodcock tend to hold fairly well, but they too can be fickle. The rule of thumb, especially during a dog's first season or two, should be to ignore all birds that flush of their own accord and those which you are unsure whether or not he has pointed. This demands self-discipline in great measure, especially if the bird happens to be the first shootable grouse of the day after three hours in the woods! It is a rule most hunters

would not be prepared to go along with, but if you are a dog man more than a hunter, as I hope you are, you'll have to make up your mind to accept it.

If you do shoot birds over a pointing dog when you cannot tell for certain whether he pointed, you may in fact be shooting birds he has flushed. And birds shot over a pointing dog that he had knowingly flushed lead directly down the slippery slope to unstaunch points and general unsteadiness. Be staunch yourself, and you'll reap the benefit in seasons to come.

Start by hunting the dog into the area where the birds have been planted, check as usual to see that the dog is staunchly holding his point, then stand on the line. Wait a few seconds and give your helper the nod to walk in and flush the bird. As the bird flies, concentrate on watching the dog, not the bird. Your helper will have noted its location when he shot it, and hopefully so will the dog. When the bird is down, wait a while as you would if it were a dummy and be ready to act, because if a break is going to occur, that's when it will happen.

Don't let the dog retrieve the first two or three birds that are shot over him, even though he remains good and steady. Have your helper walk out and pick them up in full view of the dog. As he walks out for a bird, say "Gone away" to the dog, and nothing more unless you have to. Let the dog take a sniff at each bird collected and, as you progress, walk out to pick one up yourself now and then, making quite sure he stands his ground. Now you will appreciate the value of having done this earlier with the dummies, when you allowed him to collect only the ones you wanted.

Repeat the process for another couple of sessions, leaving the check cord in place despite the fact that he's holding, because next you are going to let him do some actual bird retrieving. They will not be, for the moment, the birds just shot, but cold dead birds from the previous training session. Make sure they are clean and free of blood and have your helper carry them in a pocket or bag.

I prefer pigeons for this but naturally if up until now you have always used quail, by all means use dead quail instead. The reason for using cold dead birds at first is that it tends to discourage a young dog from "mouthing," which can sometimes

Dead-bird retrieving. As with dummies, the bird is thrown while Jason remains steady alongside . . .

. . . He's then sent for the bird . . .

. . . which he locates . . .

. . . retrieves . . .
. . . and delivers to hand.

happen when first retrieving warm, freshly shot birds.

Start by having him stand alongside you and give him several retrieves of dead birds thrown by your partner as the gun is fired. Make him wait until commanded to retrieve; also tap him lightly on the head if you used this technique with the dummies. Have him bring them right to hand and, if he's at all hesitant, adopt the same tactics as with dummy retrieving—backing away, whistling, calling him, etc.

After a couple of sessions of this, provided he has performed well, you can proceed to use the dead birds in conjunction with shooting over him after a point and when a bird has been flushed.

This time, when your partner walks in and flushes the bird, he should shoot but not to hit it. Instead he will have with him a cold dead bird which he will throw, after the shot, in full view of the dog, twenty yards or so in front. The dog's attention will then be wrested from the departing flyer onto the thrown dead one. The dog won't know the difference. Pause for the compulsory few seconds, then give the command to retrieve. After doing this another two or three times, leave it for the day. Next time out, you can fire the gun yourself but still have your helper throw the dead bird.

Only now—and I make no apologies for being so strict because

Lucky, an English setter, is given a direction signal to locate a bird . . .

. . . which he finds and brings in at speed.

that is what training is all about—may you allow him to retrieve
some birds that have actually been shot over him. Remember
the rules: your helper to do the shooting; you to watch the dog;
check line still on; a quiet pause once the bird has fallen before
you send the dog to retrieve, and praise when he delivers to you.

Two or three birds shot and retrieved in one session are
enough, and remember to let one or two fly off unscathed with
a shot fired in the air. You did this with dummies and he came
to understand it; now you're doing the same with birds, so
there's every reason to believe he'll understand this too. Like
us he must (albeit reluctantly) come to terms with the fact that
not all birds that are shot at are brought down.

Once more self-confidence will dictate to you when the check
line and choke chain can be removed, and lastly, having had
your partner shoot for you for a while, all that remains now is
for you to do the shooting yourself.

Live-bird work on planted pigeons. Gunner, a gordon setter, quartering with style.

Carry a gun yourself if you wish, but during early bird-work having a friend do the shooting is best. This allows you to concentrate fully on the dog.

Gunner makes a good solid point.
The bird is flushed and the shot taken.

Any dog which retrieves with a soft mouth is worth its weight in gold!

The bird is delivered straight to hand.

When confident of steadiness, you may do the shooting yourself. Maxi, a brittany spaniel, holds an intense point.

Moving in to flush the bird.

A successful shot.

Maxi holds, then is sent for the retrieve.
The pickup.

Nicely presented.

Bearing in mind that you're assuming two roles—i.e., dog handler and gunner—your actions on walking up to your dog when he's on point are going to be somewhat different now so we'll go through them from A to Z. First make sure that your gun is loaded (it's easily forgotten!). Approach your dog from the side or front. Give him a reminder to "whoa" as you start to kick around in the cover in front of him prior to kicking up the bird. Watch the dog carefully all the time for signs of movement. If he holds well, flush the bird but don't shoot too soon. Pause for a second or two to look at your dog and to "whoa" him again. Then swing on the bird and shoot. As the bird drops, don't dwell on where it has fallen; instead, look around immediately at the dog again to be sure he has held. Pause, unload, then send him for the retrieve.

A lot to do, you may think, but in practice it's done almost without thinking and accomplished in seconds. Take my advice and learn to do this as a routine.

What you have achieved by now, therefore, should convince you that at last you have a dog which is steady to wing and shot. There's still wild bird hunting to be done of course, which we'll get around to later. But you have now progressed through the most important and difficult stages of this fascinating (and at times frustrating!) aspect of training.

BACKING ANOTHER DOG

The term "backing" simply means stopping during the course of hunting and honoring the point of another dog.

Obviously, problems are going to arise if two dogs are being hunted together, when neither of them will stand off and back the point of the other dog. This will often result in one dog's going on point and the other, on seeing it, running in to steal the point, getting in beyond the first, and probably thereby bumping and flushing the bird. Ideally any good bird dog, on seeing another on point, should stop immediately without command and honor its bracemate's point by pointing also, whether or not it has actually got the scent. This is good manners, which as I've said repeatedly before usually comes about as a result of sound training. There are even some pointing dogs which will

honor immediately and instinctively on sight without any training being required.

Many gun dog owners rarely if ever hunt their dog in the company of another, so the importance of being able to back another
dog is not so necessary in their case. Yet to hunt a well-trained
and steady gun dog in the company of a wild-running reprobate
does no good at all. A well-disciplined dog will not teach an
ill-disciplined one good manners. On the contrary, as likely as
not the badly trained dog will cause problems in the other. A
gun dog is not trained by the simple expedient of watching
another hunting. In fact, he is likely to learn only bad habits!

However, this does not detract from the fact that, when teaching a young dog to back, the best way to do so is to work him
with an older dog, provided (and I emphasize this) the older dog
is staunch and steady and has been taught to back also. If this
is not the case, don't even consider it.

As an alternative, some trainers use a method to teach backing which involves the use of a dummy dog, or life-size cutout.
It is made by drawing the outline of a dog as though on point
on a sheet of plywood. This is then cut out and the resulting
silhouette is painted white, with a few liver or black markings
on the head and back if desired. The legs should be cut with
a sharp end so that they stick directly into the ground or, alternatively, they can be secured to a wide, flat piece of board to
keep the silhouette upright.

Let's examine these two methods to see how they work.

We will assume that you know someone who owns a really
good, well-trained dog. Ask if you can work with him for a few
sessions in order to teach yours backing. He may first want to
satisfy himself that your dog has reached a certain standard and
is ready for this. As likely as not, he'll want to see him working
to make sure you have him under control—anything else might
mess his dog up!

Approach this as you would any other training session by
planting a couple of birds. But this time be sure to put them out
in release cages as they'll hold better this way, and you will want
them to hold longer than usual for this exercise. If they weren't
caged but only hand-planted, they might flush and fly off too
soon.

Select a location in which your own dog (on the check line again) will come into sight of the other dog suddenly and unexpectedly. A hedgerow or a hollow in the field will do. Then work your dog upwind towards the other and be ready, as soon as the other dog comes into view, to "whoa" your own if necessary.

The older dog should be hunted first until he locates and goes into a good solid point. Watch your dog's reaction carefully because you may find there's an automatic slowup or he may even come to a full stop through surprise. And if gets scent of the bird, he may go on point anyway without having noticed the other dog. It is better, though, that he see the other dog and recognize what it is doing, as you do want him to react by sight in this case. Using the surprise element each time in this manner should soon give him the right idea.

If your dog doesn't stop and point right away, but instead shows interest in moving in too close to the other dog, don't let him. Step on the line, set him up, and "whoa" him.

Some dogs tend to exhibit signs of jealousy on seeing another dog on point. They cannot resist moving closer in an attempt to "steal" the point, and no amount of persuasion will change their ideas. This type of dog will never back naturally or willingly but will do so only on command, which will have to be strongly instilled.

Allow time for both dogs to hold point, then one of you should walk forward, flush the bird, and fire a blank shot. The bird must be flushed each time in order to convince your own dog that whenever he comes upon another dog pointing, there will be a bird there.

Repeat this exercise two or three times a week if you can, until he shows he's really getting the idea. Repetition, and association with the same area, should soon teach him. A couple of points each session are sufficient.

I realize that, by using the same area for two weeks or so, he'll soon learn to anticipate what's ahead, which will in turn tend to negate the surprise element. But the sudden sighting of the other dog on point, as he tops the rise or rounds the hill or hedge, is still going to have the desired effect. By this time you can expect your dog to "whoa" and honor the point of his own accord as soon as he sees the other dog. Once he is doing so,

Chips pointing on the left; Jason backing. Use of the check line is advisable until a young dog is backing reliably.

Jason is now working free of the check line.

This time it's Jason's bird. Chips honors his point.

Jason is brought in to back Chips again, but this time from an upwind position.

Now a working team. Shooting should commence on wild birds only when honoring on the part of both dogs is reliably established.

it should be safe to remove both the check line and the choke chain. Always remember to flush the bird and fire a shot each time a good point and backing have been accomplished. Don't hesitate to pick up your dog and put him back where he should be each time he moves in too close.

When you have reached the stage where he's backing consistently well, try changing the location so that he understands that this can happen anywhere, anytime. And last of all, switch things around so that your own dog works first, with the other dog doing the backing. Manners work both ways; you have to be sure your own dog doesn't react jealously when the other dog comes up, consequently causing him to move in too close on his own bird. So be ready with the "Whoa" and any other corrective measures you deem appropriate.

Don't nag or scold your dog. Just speak quietly and firmly and only when necessary. By this time you should be able to anticipate your dog's reaction under all circumstances; in fact, you should almost be able to tell what is going through his mind!

When you feel confident that a bird or two can be shot over the dog while both are pointing, give it a try. But have your original helper come back in to do the shooting so that both you and your companion can concentrate on your dogs. And, once again, go back to the check line for the first couple of birds—just in case! Remember, when a dog moves, you can get your foot down on a check line far more quickly than you can reach down and grab his collar.

Every time a bird is shot, give each dog a retrieve in turn while the other stands and honors. And the "gone away" command, each time the other dog retrieves, mustn't be forgotten.

Turning to the second method, backing the plywood model works in a similar way. The cutout should be set up in a suitable spot, taking into consideration wind direction and the surprise factor as before. A quail or pigeon is placed in a release cage in such a position that the model appears realistically to be pointing it.

Hunt your dog up in precisely the same way you would if you were using the other dog. This time, though, when your dog stops and goes on point, have your helper approach the model, release the bird, and fire a shot from the pistol. Then, after waiting a few seconds for the bird to disappear, and at the time you heel your dog away, have your helper kick over the model as though it too had left the scene. Such details are important to the deception.

Repeat the process several times in the same location, then, if all goes well, move to a different area. Conclude as before by shooting a few birds over the model to allow your dog to retrieve.

Strange though it may seem, this method of teaching a dog to back can be very effective. You will probably be surprised by how your dog reacts to the model. But try to avoid allowing your dog to get close to the model if you can, thereby preserving the illusion.

You must also make an effort to hunt your dog downwind as well as the easy way, i.e., upwind. This applies whether you're using a trained dog or the cutout. If he's downwind of the other dog when he sights it and he still honors, then you definitely know that he's doing so by sight alone and not by the aid of scent too.

Although by now he's backing another dog well, bear in mind that so far it's only on planted birds. He has not yet had any experience hunting wild birds, and the difference can be considerable. I think it is vital that he have at least one season hunting alone, to get to know how to handle wild birds, before he starts hunting in the company of another dog. More backing sessions should be undertaken the following summer to reinforce the training before his second season, when you can consider hunting him with another dog—provided that dog is as well trained as he is.

What would then be more enjoyable for you and your dog than to go with the friend and the dog that you taught backing with?

THE "SIT" AND THE "DOWN"

With pointing dogs I prefer to leave the "sit" and "down" exercises until late in training and certainly until after they have learned to hold points staunchly. If the "sit" and the "down" are taught before staunchness, you may find that a dog will develop the habit of sitting or going down as you approach him while he is on point. This should be avoided at all costs. It doesn't apply to all dogs, of course, but in general the premature initiation of either can in fact start this off.

Both the "sit" and the "down" are easily taught and they can in fact be instilled at the same time while walking a dog to heel.

Take your dog out into the yard or field and slip on a nylon pocket leash, assuming he already walks to heel well. As you are walking along with the dog on your left, stop suddenly, give the command "Sit," and at the same time pull up gently on the leash while pressing down lightly on the dog's haunches with your other hand. This will push him into the sitting position. Let him sit there a while, then walk on with the command "Heel," stopping to repeat the "sit" exercise every twenty yards or so until the slightest touch on the haunches will cause him to sit down. You'll be surprised how quickly this will occur. After only two or three sessions of this for twenty minutes each time, he'll be sitting without any touch at all.

Once he's got the idea of sitting you can start to incorporate the "down" command too. This again is best taught while he's walking to heel and should be done in the following way. As you're walking along, suddenly say "Down" and point to the ground in front of him; at the same time, place your left hand on his back close to the shoulders and push down and to one side. This will tend to overbalance him a little and he should go down with no trouble. He may at first try to get up as you straighten up, so be ready for this. Say "Down" again, point to the ground, and push him back. Having got accustomed to the pressure on his haunches for the "sit," he's unlikely to resist the same force applied to his shoulders for the "down," and he will soon understand what you want.

Each time you have made him go down, allow him to lie there for thirty seconds or so before saying "Heel" to him and walking on; then repeat the exercise as you did with the "sit." Don't get into the habit, as many people do, of first telling a dog to sit, then proceeding directly to "down." This will lead to confusion. Be specific and clear as to which action you want—"sit" or "down," but not both.

When he's going down without your touching his back, you will find that he will have started to react to your hand signal in front of him pointing to the ground. Try it, and you'll find

Teaching the "sit." Place hand under jaw (or pull up on leash); at the same time, press down on haunches while giving the command.

Jason sits . . .

. . . and is praised.

Teaching the "down." With the leash still on, Muppy is first placed in the down position . . .

. . . then is given a reminder as the trainer walks away.

that if you suddenly stop and point to the ground, without a word of command, he'll go down just as though you had told him to. This is the value of the hand signal. In time, provided you're insistent on it, even when the dog is several yards from you, if you point to the ground he'll know what you mean and comply.

You can start to walk away from him now, leaving him lying there. There's no need to say "Stay." You've already told him "Down" and he's complying. If he does get up or show signs of restlessness, just repeat the command "Down," make sure he doesn't move, then walk off and around him.

RETRIEVING FROM WATER

I have already outlined in chapter 4 how best to introduce a dog to water. As I stated then, there are many dogs of the various pointing breeds that simply hate it or at best tolerate it. However, if you own a dog that has really enjoyed swimming and retrieving a dummy from the water as a youngster, here are some tips on doing more advanced water work, this time using birds, while maintaining the dog's facility for sitting steady.

So far the only bird retrieving I have discussed has related to

Water work using dead birds. Gunner sits nicely at heel . . .

. . . while the bird is thrown . . .

. . . He is then given the verbal command and signal to "fetch" . . .

. . . and he enters the water at a good speed . . .

. . . heading directly for the bird.

There can be no mistaking his love for retrieving . . .

. . . whether on land or water.

upland hunting. This involved, first, thrown dead birds, followed by live birds which were pointed, then flushed and shot.

As mentioned before, choose warmer weather as your dog will enter the water much more willingly. I suggest using cold dead pigeons as they tend to show up well on the water. And use a pond with a gradually sloping bank if you can, rather than one he has to jump into.

He knows what "Sit" means now so have him sit alongside you a few yards back from the water's edge. Tell him "Whoa," watch him carefully so you'll see any signs of him breaking, and throw the bird out into the water—just far enough so that he has to swim a few yards to get it, once out of his depth. It is not necessary at the moment to fire a shot. Before you send him, pause as you would if you were doing this on land; then, giving him a hand signal in the direction of the bird, command "Fetch." The fact that it's a bird he's seen thrown should increase his enthusiasm; if as a puppy he enjoyed water, then he certainly will now.

As he gets the bird and turns in the water, give a few pips on the whistle in the same way you would for the recall and then, as his feet touch terra firma once more and he begins to wade out, walk backwards away from him in an effort to keep him coming with the bird. Run back if you have to.

With some dogs, there is no way you can ever prevent them from first putting down a bird before they shake themselves. A problem arises only if he refuses to pick it up again after he has shaken. If he doesn't pick up the bird again to bring it on, try wading in so that you get the bird from him while he is still swimming. You can then gradually decrease the distance you wade in if this appears to be working.

With some dogs this tactic will work well and they will start to hand over before shaking, but with many, they will revert to their old habit once on dry land again and you will just have to accept things that way. I have found, however that if it's a live duck he's retrieving under actual shooting conditions, it is extremely unlikely he will put the bird down after one or two he's released have dived back into the water and disappeared. At this, a dog will usually start holding on!

Sometimes shackled ducks can help. These are live mallard

tied in such a way that they can't fly or dive. They're not shot but are simply used for the dog to retrieve. It may prove difficult for you to get ducks for this purpose though, so if you do want to have your dog retrieve a few, contact a professional trainer of retrievers. He'll probably have some and be willing to help you out.

After two or three sessions of throwing the birds yourself, you can recruit your helper to throw them from a greater distance, this time with a shot fired too. You can if you wish try shooting a few flyers also, but you will have to set this up carefully as most pigeons, for example, tend to swing back when flown out over water, which may spoil things. For all practical purposes, in my opinion, just as effective a job can be done with dead birds. There's less chance of anything going wrong and you can throw them exactly where you want them.

When your dog is marking and retrieving singles confidently, there's no reason why you shouldn't use two birds for double retrieves. While this really is in the realm of the retriever, a keen retrieving pointing dog should become adept at this too.

Try the double retrieve on a calm day if you can because if the water is choppy, by the time he has retrieved the first bird thrown out, the second may have drifted back to the bank or out beyond his sight. For the moment at least, it's important that he be able to see clearly each bird as he is sent for it. When he has brought back the first bird, have him sit again alongside you, give the hand signal in the direction of the second bird, and send him again. For a while he may have forgotten the second bird and, consequently, react by standing up and looking or milling around on the edge of the water. If this happens, call him in to you again and try a second time. If absolutely necessary, throw a pebble in close to where the bird is in order to attract the dog's attention. Allow a little time and show patience and he'll eventually get the idea, provided that from now on you give him a double every time and, if possible, have him retrieve them in the same order until it has clicked in his mind.

Double retrieving is good for any gun dog. Not only does it improve marking ability; it helps improve his memory too.

9

Hunting Your Dog

FIRST TRIPS AFIELD

The training you have carried out has all been done for the specific purpose of instilling in your dog sound discipline and good manners. And all the bird work so far has been with pen-reared birds and therefore of an artificial nature.

The time has now arrived when you can start to hunt him properly on wild birds and, as I have already stated, herein lies a difference.

When hunting wild birds, whether they be grouse, woodcock, quail, or pheasant, your dog will have to learn something he so far knows little or nothing about, and this is *caution*. Wild birds survive only because their reaction to the sound of approaching danger is fast and decisive. Pen-reared birds possess this instinct, of course, but to a far lesser degree since they have throughout their life, until released, been accustomed to the presence and sound of humans. Wild birds have not. To them human beings and dogs mean only danger and they react accordingly with remarkable speed.

It is in part for this reason that I mentioned much earlier in this book the advisability of handling your dog quietly while training him. I stated that there should be no need to continually yell and bellow when handling any dog which has been trained properly in the first place. Shouting indicates lack of control, while quiet handling denotes precisely the opposite. If you have accepted this advice, then its value will be repaid tenfold now that you are starting to hunt. And the reason? Nothing disturbs wild game more than the sound of the human voice. Quiet commands and the use of the whistle will result in far more shooting. Conversely, handling a pointing dog on wild birds in the manner in which they are handled in field trials would almost certainly result in your having blank days repeatedly, especially when hunting grouse and woodcock.

I mentioned the use of a collar bell before and for a very specific reason. A dog should wear a bell, not because it sounds nice, but so that, if hunting in particularly dense cover, he can be located when he stops and goes on point. Even though your dog may be a reliably close worker, certain woodland conditions make it impossible for a handler to keep his dog in sight at all times. But when a bell has been tinkling away all the time he's been on the move and it suddenly stops, he may be on point.

Training having progressed well, Natasha is worked on pheasants on a cold, windy day. She locates and makes a nice solid point.

Having given a reminder to "whoa," the author goes in to flush the bird . . .

. . . and a cock pheasant rockets upwards.

The retrieve completed. Praise should always be given for good work.

Natasha's first pheasant.

This gives you at least an inkling of where he is. That is the entire purpose of the bell.

You may be tempted to hunt your dog just as soon as the shooting-preserve season opens, which in many of the Northeastern states is September 1st. However, I would advise that you wait at least until October. By then the weather will be cooler and there will be the beginnings of frost to help flatten cover and improve scent. Hunting pheasant on hot days in September will do nothing to improve your dog's ability. The cover will be too dense and green, and likely as not, scenting will be poor also.

Many people tend to worry about their dogs in winter. Forget it! Dogs love it and behave like puppies in the snow. The time to be concerned, and to be extremely careful about hunting any dog, is when it's hot and humid. Heat prostration is an ever-present danger in hot weather and if a dog succumbs to it out in the field, unless you happen to be close to a shaded, cool stream in which the dog can be immersed, the chances are good that it will kill him quickly. It's just not worth taking the risk. Never hunt any dog for long in hot weather and always have a good supply of drinking water for him.

For the first few hunting trips I think it best to ask your partner to come along with you to do the shooting. I have already explained in regard to training the reason for this, namely, so that you can concentrate fully on the dog at the crucial time when flushing and shooting take place. If you are free from the responsibility of the gun, your whole concentration can be centered on the dog.

Remember, training routine can never be relaxed, especially during the first season's hunting. Your dog is still learning (and so are you) and it is essential that you be aware of this. Your reaction and that of your partner are also going to be different than when you were working the dog on the training field. By this I mean that now you will not know when birds are going to be encountered. With planted birds, you knew at least approximately where each one was and you could therefore anticipate what was going to happen. Now each bird located will be a surprise and the adrenaline will be flowing faster. And whether you realize it or not, this state of mind is transmitted to your dog.

Woodcock tend to hold fairly well for a dog. They are as a rule less "spooky" than grouse and more cooperative for a pointing dog. Grouse on the other hand, particularly in the more populous states where disturbance by man is more prevalent, will flush and whirr away at the crack of a twig, invariably out of sight beyond the next clump of laurel. It is possible to fly several grouse in the course of a morning's hunting, yet of those raised, maybe only half will actually be seen for a brief second or two and of these only a small fraction will be in a position to be shootable. Anyone who limits out on grouse has a good dog and can be justifiably satisfied with his marksmanship too. Every bird bagged is well deserved.

A pointing dog has to learn to exercise caution when hunting grouse and he will gain this knowledge only by making mistakes. He'll accidentally bump birds (flush them by mistake) but only by doing this from time to time will he learn to get "sneaky." You must remember never to shoot birds disturbed in this way, no matter how tempting it may be. Flushing birds is for spaniels and retrievers, not for bird dogs.

The value of having insisted on close working right from

Grouse hunting. Natasha, a Hungarian vizsla, quarters ahead in the woods.

A bird is located in windfall branches . . .

. . . and a snap shot brings it down.

The last grouse of the season.

puppy on will be appreciated even more now. A dog working far out in woodland is of no use whatever, whereas one that keeps a visual check on your whereabouts—and there are many that do—is worth his weight in grouse!

Self-discipline and the desire to have the best possible dog you could wish for should be uppermost in your mind. To achieve this, you're going to have to give up opportunities for shots now and then. You can't have it both ways.

If it's pheasants you are hunting (and for many people there is no alternative), bear in mind what I have said about not allowing your dog to go out to retrieve, the first time, a wounded cockbird. Hunting on a local shooting preserve is a good introduction, as you can ask that hen birds only be released, so he can learn to carry them first.

You simply have to accept that if pheasant hunting is going to be your main sport, sooner or later your dog will start bird trailing—it's inevitable. Pheasants will run rather than fly if they can and, when they do, they are a great temptation to any good dog. Some pointing dog owners don't like this and will keep their dogs off pheasants for this very reason. They claim that running pheasants, more than any other bird, result in a dog's becoming less staunch on point. I suppose this to a certain extent is true and I do agree that if a dog is kept off pheasants for its first season, and instead worked only on grouse, woodcock, or quail, the chances of this happening will lessen.

However, I still think a lot of good sport can be had with a pointing dog on pheasants and I certainly suggest that, once he's handling other birds well, you give him the opportunity to work them too—that is, unless you happen to worship at the altar of grouse and woodcock and prefer to hunt them to the exclusion of all else.

Many dogs eventually learn to listen for a pheasant running through cover; in order to counteract this, they will hook around the bird in a semi-circle to cut off its escape and make it hunker down again. Some dogs can do this very quickly and can hold a bird well until the gun is in position. This is learned only by experience, though, and can be a great asset provided the dog still realizes that, just as long as the bird stays still, he must stand and hold his point staunchly.

With pheasants especially, don't be tempted to send your dog for a long retrieve on a lightly hit bird. He may get into the area of the fall (where the bird went down) and then have to finish up chasing a weak-flying bird for a considerable distance to catch it. If your dog is far away in deep cover and obviously out of sight, you don't know what's going on and therefore have no control over the situation. Instead, you should mark the bird well, then walk your dog at heel into the area downwind of the fall. He should be told to hunt again in the usual way and this time, when he comes across it, since he is close to you and controllable, a chase is less likely to occur.

When hunting quail, particularly wild ones, your dog will

have to get used to multiple flushes. This can apply even on a shooting preserve where pen-raised quail have been released, as it doesn't take too long for birds to call one another together. There really isn't a lot one can do during training to prepare a dog for this, other than to carry two or three extra birds in a pocket or bag. They can then be released to fly off one at a time while the dog is actually still pointing a caged bird. If this is to be at all effective, they must be released when he's actually on point as this is how birds would rise were he pointing a covey. He will naturally be surprised and puzzled at first, so the check cord may be necessary just to ensure he doesn't break and chase due to the added excitement. Be quite sure though not to let him see you releasing the birds. If this is done several times, he should soon get the idea and be better able to cope when actually hunted later.

One's hunting companions also should be chosen with care! The best person to shoot over your dog is obviously the friend or member of your family who did so during training, as he already knows not to shoot a bird that flies without having been pointed; and more important, how to handle a gun safely. Anyone who doesn't is not fit to go hunting with under any circumstances. There are those people who, out of excitement, shoot far too soon at a rising bird and consequently too low. Avoid them like the plague, as you may finish up with a dead dog! It has happened.

People who want to handle your dog for you can also be a pain in the neck. They just won't keep quiet and can't resist telling your dog to "hunt 'em out" every few seconds. Or they keep whistling to him to draw him away to hunt other cover. A dog needs one handler and one handler only—that's you. Tell this type if he wants to handle a dog to get his own! And be quite sure to make clear to the man who, having shot a bird, runs in to do the retrieving himself, that that's the dog's job. It's the dog's reward for pointing it—not his for shooting it!

WORKING DOGS AT A SHOOTING PRESERVE

In addition to hunting and shooting over your dog yourself, it is possible by guiding at a local shooting preserve or private club shoot to gain valuable experience on considerably more birds than would otherwise be the case.

Serious consideration should be given to doing this if you think it's a form of sport you would enjoy, but I advise that it would be perhaps best to hunt and shoot over your dog for the first season yourself, then consider guiding with him from his second. Too many birds in a dog's first season may be upsetting, especially in relation to steadiness. A young dog can get overexcited and start to break and run in if too many birds are shot over him in too short a time. So make sure he can walk before he starts to run!

We will assume therefore that your dog has had a full season hunting wild birds and has done a good job for you, remaining steady and obedient. There are bound to be some wrinkles that need ironing out, so some refresher training through the summer months prior to the start of the following season should be undertaken, using precisely the same methods as during the previous year. It's just a way of making certain that everything is retained. It's a long time for any dog from the end of one season to the start of the next.

If in his second season you think he's up to being used for guiding, go to a club or preserve in the area and speak with the manager. Tell him all about your dog and, since he has probably heard similar stories from others whose dogs proved to be rogues, offer to bring your dog for a demonstration. This may well clinch things.

Most clubs and preserves pay the guides for their services, of course, in addition to which the "guns" on a walkup shoot are expected to tip also. Maybe you won't be paid until the manager is satisfied with the job you're doing but, provided things go right, you no doubt will be in time. Good handlers are hard to come by.

At most shoots the day's program takes two forms. Many start in the morning with a tower shoot. This is a bird release, usually pheasant, sometimes mallard, sometimes a mixture of both. The birds are released from either a high wooden tower, which is usually well-screened back in the trees on high ground, or a hilltop in the woods. Two or three hundred birds may be released in the course of two or three hours. And the guns, maybe

A pheasant pen at a hunting club.

A typical release tower.

A tower shoot is in progress; pheasants are being released. A "gun" stands by his blind and the author is handling Jason.

After a specified number of birds, usually ten, have been released, the guns move around to the next blind. Jason is marking a bird which has fallen to the right of the blind.

The walkup after the tower shoot is over. Jason on point. The guns move in ready for the flush.

For reasons of safety, only two guns shoot.

Outside the clubhouse with a few birds in the bag.

fourteen or fifteen in all, are stationed at predetermined positions, each marked by a stake bearing a number. These stations either completely encircle the tower or half-circle it, each station being at least two hundred yards or so from the release point. The guns draw for position before the shoot starts and, after each release of ten or twelve birds, they all move around one position. Due to wind direction or the position of the sun, the shooting is likely to be better in some places than others; moving around evens things up for everyone in turn.

Advantage is taken of the lie of the land when a tower shoot is first laid out in an attempt to have the birds fly as high as possible over the guns. This doesn't usually work as well as driven-pheasant shooting in Britain, although the idea of tower shoots is to simulate this. In Britain young pheasants are released to the woods by the gamekeepers when seven weeks old. They gradually become self-sufficient and wild by the time driven bird shooting commences in late October or early November. Beaters then drive them from the woods over the waiting guns and, at most shoots, they fly high and fast and present difficult targets, especially after the first two or three shoots have been held. And the reason for this is simple—they know where they are flying to! They've had several months of living wild and roving the estate and they know it inside out. In contrast, tower-released birds do not know where they are flying to, so tend to land sooner, thereby presenting as a rule somewhat lower targets.

We'll return now to the job of the dog handler at a tower shoot. While the shoot is in progress, several handlers are positioned at points behind the circle of guns in order that they can see the shooting taking place and mark the birds accurately that have been shot. For a shoot with this many guns you will usually find there are five or six handlers, each responsible for a couple of gun positions. Usually the picking up is done by handlers working retrievers or springer spaniels, which I consider to be the dogs best suited for this. However, there is absolutely no reason why you should not use your German shorthair or brittany or vizsla, or any of the versatile pointer/retriever breeds, for this also—provided (and only provided) your dog is a good, reliable retriever. If he isn't, then you simply can't consider using him for this.

Your dog should stand or sit alongside you and remain steady and quiet during the shooting. Due to the training you have given him, he should stay steady despite the number of birds flying about, but for the first shoot or two, I suggest slipping a leash on just to make sure, since this is another new experience for him. Any birds that fall dead in front of the guns should be left until the release is over and the guns are changing stations; then they can be retrieved. Those that fall behind the guns (where the dog handlers are) and within the area you are responsible for can be collected by you and the dog at any time, provided you are sure he will listen obediently to your commands and whistle while the shooting is still going on. He should do so because of the steadiness-to-shot training you gave him. When collected, the birds are normally left by the handler, at the end of the shoot, at the closest gun's station, where they are collected by someone in a vehicle.

Until your dog gets accustomed to all this, be careful about sending him for an obviously wounded runner. Never send your dog while the bird is still in sight, as to do so encourages chasing. Wait until the birds gets into cover, then walk up with the dog to where you last saw it, and cast him off to hunt for it. As the bird is wounded, more likely than not it won't go far once in cover, but will quickly tuck itself in and hide. Your chances of recovering the bird are better using these tactics. If you prefer to wait until the shooting is over and everyone is moving around again, then do so. You're the handler and no one can tell you how to handle your own dog.

There is a certain amount of conflict when working a pointing dog in this way, whereas with a flushing dog there is none. Now you are requiring no pointing of him, just retrieving, but these are birds which he himself has seen shot and fall. He's sitting alongside you, remember, and you have already done somewhat similar exercises in training. Provided you send him only for those birds down and dead and you remember to exercise caution in the manner I have described on those that are runners, you will do no harm with the dog at all.

Never send your dog for birds which you are not certain have been hit. Just think and use common sense. This is precisely why I recommended that you shoot over the dog yourself for the first season before considering preserve guiding. He's nearly three years old by now and, because of the training and experience you have previously given him, you should have no problem.

The second part of the day, after lunch, usually takes the form of a walkup shoot. This is where two or three of the guns are guided by a dog handler in order to hunt up those birds that have been missed during the tower shoot. If they shot sixty percent of the birds in the tower shoot they did well, so there are sure to be quite a few birds still out there.

If you are asked to accompany four guns, as will sometimes be the case, two should walk with you, one on each side, to do the shooting while the other two walk along behind with their weapons unloaded. Change-around times can be amicably agreed upon.

You as the handler are in charge of the hunt, so start by telling the guns what you intend doing, how your dog will work, and what you expect of them. By this I mean there should be a couple of shots each at one bird and no more. No low shooting should be countenanced, which means you want to see daylight under the bird as it tops the trees before a shot is fired.

Most people start to shoot far too soon anyway, and there can be no valid excuse for shooting a dog.

Ask them to listen carefully to your directions once the dog goes on point, and insist that they keep quiet while you walk in to flush the bird. Also, shotguns are to be opened while the dog is retrieving. Most participants are very sporting and rarely if ever will you find anyone objecting to anything politely suggested. But do not under any circumstances tolerate dangerous shooting. If you encounter this, then tell them that's it, the shoot is over, and go back to the clubhouse and report to the manager. No shoot, private or public, will tolerate this and if your reasons are valid the club will back you up.

Most walkups after a tower release last a couple of hours or thereabouts and the company and sport can be very enjoyable. In addition, your dog is gaining valuable experience. You're not encumbered with a gun yourself, so your concentration can be fully on him, thereby enabling you to correct any tendency on his part to step out of line.

On days when no tower shoot is held, only walkups take place. Either pheasants, chukar partridge, quail, or a combination of all these is released in the morning, and away you go later with your party to hunt. These hunts may last three hours or so, depending upon the enthusiasm and physical endurance of your clients.

So give it some thought and, if you think you might enjoy working your dog this way for a day or so a week, ask around and try to get started somewhere.

Have fun, be a good sportsman, and try to return in full measure all the love your dog gives to you.

Index